Vatzlav

A PLAY IN 77 SCENES

Slawomir Mrozek

Translated from the Polish by Ralph Manheim

JONATHAN CAPE
THIRTY BEDFORD SQUARE
LONDON

Translated from the Polish *Vatzlav*
© 1970 by Karl H. Henssel Verlag
English version first published in Great Britain 1972 by
Jonathan Cape Ltd, 30 Bedford Square, London WC1
English version © 1970 by Grove Press, Inc., New York

ISBN Paperback 0 224 00608 8
      Hardback 0 224 00609 6

Printed and bound in Great Britain
by Richard Clay (The Chaucer Press), Ltd
Bungay, Suffolk

Vatzlav

CHARACTERS

VATZLAV

MR BAT

MRS BAT

BOBBIE

QUAIL

SASSAFRAS

THE GENIUS

JUSTINE

OEDIPUS

BARBARO

THE LACKEY

THE GUIDE

THE OFFICER

A VOICE

SOLDIERS

THE EXECUTIONER

CHORUS OF THE PEOPLE

VOICE OF A MAN OF THE PEOPLE

VOICE OF A WOMAN OF THE PEOPLE

SCENE 1

The stage, consisting of a platform inclined towards the audience, is empty.
Half-light. Thunder and lightning. VATZLAV appears upstage and climbs up on the platform. He is a powerfully built man in his forties, with blond hair. He is wearing a white collarless shirt of coarse material and trousers with frayed edges reaching halfway between his knees and ankles. He is barefoot.
He steps forward and speaks to the audience.

VATZLAV. I was a slave and now I'm shipwrecked,
        An outcast slave and now a castaway.
        Condemned to slavery, set free by ship-
           wreck,
        Finding, when all was lost, my freedom, yet
        Too lost and battered to enjoy my freedom –
        Maybe a rest would help.
    (*He sits down on the ground.*)
In the storm today a slave ship foundered off the coast. I don't know what coast this is, but it must be far from my country. Taking advantage of the disaster, I swam ashore – well, to tell the truth, the sea threw me up on the sand. My companions were drowned.

A VOICE (*off, right – the indications 'right' and 'left' are always from the point of view of the audience*). He-elp!

VATZLAV. Not all of them apparently. Hey, you alive?

THE VOICE. I'm drowning.

VATZLAV. Just what I said. He's drowning like the rest. Me, I'm saved. By decision of Providence. If there is a Providence. There must be, because if there's been a decision, it must come from someplace. If it was a decision. Let it go. It's facts that count, and the fact is I haven't been drowned.

THE VOICE. I'm drowning.

VATZLAV. Quit the bragging. You should have seen me when I was drowning.

THE VOICE. Help!

VATZLAV. I'd go to his rescue if there was a Providence that meant to save the poor bastard. But it doesn't look like it. On the contrary. It looks as if Providence had made up its mind to let him drown, and who am I to meddle with its decisions? Assuming, of course, that there is a Providence, and in his case I'll bet money there is.

THE VOICE. Oh, oh!

VATZLAV. That proves it. The man's in trouble.

THE VOICE. Countryman!

VATZLAV. Countryman? Yes, he is from my country. I could save him if Providence weren't against it. Suppose I bucked Providence? Then what? I'd have a witness to my slavery. Wherever I went, his eyes would say to me: I remember, old friend.

Once freed, a single slave can forget. A second slave won't let him. Conclusion : Providence wants the second to drown so he can't interfere with the first.

THE VOICE. Friend!

VATZLAV. Friend? If you're my friend, leave me alone. Does a friend stand in a friend's way? What kind of a friend is it that keeps reminding you: you were a slave? You're no friend of mine and you're no friend of freedom if you insist on living and poisoning other people's freedom. If that fellow that's calling me is a real friend, he ought to realize that I don't need him. (*He stands up.*) New life, I salute you!

THE VOICE. Traitor!

VATZLAV. Traitor? Who have I betrayed? Did I promise anybody not to escape if I could? No. My guards swore I'd never escape. If I've escaped, it's my guards that haven't kept their word. Or did I swear to my fellow slaves that I'd go to the bottom with them if the ship was wrecked? No, there was no such agreement between us. Who could I betray? Only the Providence that has chosen me. That I will never do. I will go to meet my destiny, and I will say . . .

THE VOICE. I'm dying!

VATZLAV. . . . Here I am. Destiny, you want me to be free . . . But come to think of it, what for . . . What can you do with freedom? . . . I'd better think this over. (*He paces the stage.*) What do free men do?

(*He counts on his fingers.*) They make money, they win honour and glory. They've done it since the beginning of the world. Slaves are the only people who don't, because they're forbidden to. I see. Providence is showing me the way. Providence wants me to be rich, powerful and happy. And you think you can prevent me, you envious chunk of fish bait? (*He raises one arm heavenward as though to grasp a hand that is held out to him.*) Okay, it's a deal. (*He puts out two fingers and swears.*) Providence, I swear to you you will not be disappointed, you can count on me.

(*Thunder and lightning*)

There's the answer. That's our pact.

THE VOICE. Save me!

VATZLAV. Try to see it my way, old man. I've sworn an oath. (*He listens. Silence.*) He's caught on. No more witness. Nobody to prevent me from starting a new life. Nobody knows me here. If anybody asks me who I am and where I come from, I'll introduce myself as a traveller of noble family. Isn't it my right? Suffering ennobles; after all they've put me through, I've got the makings of several princes with enough left over for a good-sized duke. In our country they say all foreigners are of noble family. It must be true, because in our country there's nothing but riffraff. Since foreigners aren't us, they must be rich and noble.

(*Upstage appears* VATZLAV'*s double, a dummy*

> rolling on the ground as though buffeted by
> waves.)

You still here? Get away! You belong in the ocean.

> (*The double rolls up to* VATZLAV'*s feet*.)

Is he stubborn! (*Kicks him*.) If he's dead, why
can't he sink? Why can't he lie quietly on the
bottom? What will people think if they see me
in such company? A stiff. And a low-class stiff
at that. (*He takes the dummy by the feet and draws
him to the 'shore'*.) How can I prove he's no rela-
tion? Somebody's coming. Say, get a look at that
rig. He must be a duke.

SCENE 2

Enter from the left the LACKEY *in violet livery and
white stockings. He is carrying a tray with two glasses
of champagne on it. Seeing* VATZLAV *and the drowned
man, he stops.*

VATZLAV. Morning, Duke ...

> (*He bows very low, the* LACKEY *bows too. He
> looks at the drowned man*.)

Look, your highness, look at the pretty seagull.

> (*He points to the sky, the* LACKEY *raises his eyes*.)

Why look at the ground when the sky is so
beautiful?

13

(*The* LACKEY *looks down at the drowned man.*)
Look, Duke, I'm a great dancer. (*He does a few dance-steps and leaps.*

(*The* LACKEY *watches him but soon turns his eyes towards the drowned man.*)
... Hm. He prefers the stiff. Is the stiff better than me? What's so interesting about *him*? ... Look, Duke. If you must look at the ground, look ... a shell. Here. (*He picks up an imaginary shell.*) ... Isn't it lovely?

(*The* LACKEY *bows, so does* VATZLAV. *The* LACKEY *goes out left.*)

SCENE 3

VATZLAV *tosses the imaginary shell after the* LACKEY, *then bows ironically.*

VATZLAV. You call that a duke? He didn't sock me in the jaw. If he'd kicked me, at least, or insulted me. No, not a word. He's a fraud. I suppose they're all frauds in this country. They won't fool me again. I'll show 'em who's noble around here. (*To the drowned man*) You again? Split. Bury yourself. Heave-ho! (*He drags the dummy to the shore and throws it into the water.*)

SCENE 4

Enter from left MR and MRS BAT, both in their forties. He in black evening clothes and top hat. White gloves and spats. In one hand he is holding a black cane with a white handle, in the other a glass of champagne. He is smoking a cigar. MRS BAT is ostentatiously beautiful. Pink crinoline, very low at the neck. Complicated hairdo, lots of jewellery. In one hand an open parasol, in the other a glass of champagne.

MR BAT. Ho, my good man. Have you seen a corpse by any chance?

VATZLAV. A what?

MR BAT. I hear a drowned man has been washed up on the beach.

VATZLAV. Who?

MR BAT. He seems to be deaf.

MRS BAT. Or drunk. Foreigners are often drunk.

MR BAT. A corpse. I wish to see it.

VATZLAV. See it?

MR BAT. If he's not deaf, he's crazy.

MRS BAT. Quite possibly. Foreigners are often crazy.

VATZLAV. See it? Down on your knees. Kiss the dust and do homage. That's what you can do.

MR BAT. I'm losing patience.

MRS BAT. My dear sir, my husband's question was prompted by pure kindness. If his words have ruffled you, do control your anger and answer politely. I too should like to know.

VATZLAV. He's fortunate in having a charming lady to intercede for him. I'd have strangled him. But now listen, both of you, pay close attention, or I can't answer for myself. (*He takes* MR BAT's *cigar and smokes with voluptuous pleasure.*) Our ship sank in the storm today. Do you know what a ship is?

MRS BAT. We choose to ignore that question.

VATZLAV. You don't know. If you never saw our ship, you haven't any idea what a ship really is. Fifty masts. So many sails there was room for thirty winds at once, and no crowding. As for the guns, you couldn't even count them. Every day we tossed two or three of them overboard just for the hell of it, for the splash, and there were always plenty left. The prow was pure gold.

MRS BAT. Gold?

(VATZLAV *takes the glass from* MR BAT's *hand, drinks a swallow of champagne and gives back the glass.*)

VATZLAV. It was a royal ship. It belonged to a king. Down on your knees! He was a big dictator.

MRS BAT. How big?

VATZLAV. The biggest in the world. We sailed the seven seas and wherever the nations saw our flag they bowed down to it.

MRS BAT. Why did they do that?

VATZLAV. Because he liked it.

MRS BAT. Where is he now?

VATZLAV (*pointing at the ground*). Here, in this tomb.
     Oh, poor Daddy!

MRS BAT. Daddy?

VATZLAV. I am his son. O cruel sea! An orphan's tears
     are saltier than your waters and more abundant.
     I will drown you, O sea, in my ocean.

MRS BAT. How bereaved he is!

VATZLAV. Thank you, ma'am.

MR BAT. He must be lying.

VATZLAV. Take care how you speak to the king's son.

MRS BAT. But how did you escape?

VATZLAV. We fought the tempest, but in vain. The
                waves
          Beat down upon the deck. I saw the ship
          Was sinking. My first thought was for the
                king
          My father. Daddy, climb up on my back,
          I'll save you. Thus I leapt into the sea
          And like a dolphin cleft the angry waves.
     (*He makes swimming movements.*)
          For me to swim ashore was child's play.
                Daddy,
          I said, alight. But he lay motionless.
          I turned my head. No, no. I can't go on.

MRS BAT. But he couldn't have drowned. What
     happened?

VATZLAV. Poisoned.

MRS BAT. Poisoned in mid-ocean?

VATZLAV. I was rocking and pitching. He took some

seasick tablets. Alas, he took too many. Don't make
me go on, it's too painful.

MR BAT. And the ship?

VATZLAV. It sank.

MR BAT. Such a magnificent ship. It doesn't seem possible.

VATZLAV. There was a hole.

MR BAT. In such a beautiful ship?

VATZLAV. The most beautiful hole ever seen.

MR BAT. What shall we do with him?

MRS BAT. Give him a few coppers.

VATZLAV. What! Coppers for a king's son?

MR BAT. You see. He refuses.

VATZLAV. Maybe if you said silver.

MRS BAT. The poor man!

MR BAT (*taking his wife's arm*). I've given him my
cigar.

　　(*They move to the left.*)

VATZLAV. Hey! What about that bread?

MR BAT. He can smoke it.

VATZLAV (*runs after them and bars the way*). I'm not
asking for any presents. (*He holds out the cigar to
MR BAT.*) Here. I'll sell it to you.

MR BAT. Thank you, I have more.

VATZLAV. Couldn't you give me a job?

MR BAT. I don't employ persons of good family.

VATZLAV. I'm practically nothing on my mother's
side. She was a cook.

MRS BAT. Haven't you some little job for him?

MR BAT (*stopping*). What can you do?

18

VATZLAV. Everything.

MR BAT. That's too much. (*They start off again.*)

VATZLAV. No, no, not everything. I can do certain things.

MR BAT (*stopping*). For instance?

VATZLAV. I can cheer. (*He claps his hands.*) Long live! Long live!

MR BAT. Who?

VATZLAV. Anybody.

MR BAT. What else?

VATZLAV. Or ... (*He shouts.*) Down with! Down with! ... I can do that too.

MR BAT. Down with who?

VATZLAV. You're the boss.

MR BAT. Not interested. (*They start off again.*)

VATZLAV (*barring their path*). I can imitate animals. (*He imitates a rooster.*)

MR BAT. You're out of tune.

(VATZLAV *barks.*)

That's better.

VATZLAV. I can roar too.

MR BAT (*stopping*). Roar? Let's hear you.

(VATZLAV *roars.*)

Hm, not bad.

VATZLAV. You mean maybe ...

MR BAT. I'll see what I can do.

(MRS BAT *whispers in his ear.*)

... But will he make the grade?

VATZLAV. I'll make the grade. Don't worry.

MR BAT. Get down on all fours.

(VATZLAV *complies.*)

What do you think?

MRS BAT. I think he's lovely.

MR BAT. Trot.

(VATZLAV *trots about on all fours.*)

Good. You're hired.

VATZLAV. Thanks, boss.

MR BAT. From now on you're a bear.

VATZLAV. I'd rather be a hound.

MR BAT. I have a large pack, but there's nothing to hunt. I need game.

VATZLAV. You mean ... ? Exactly what will I have to do?

MR BAT. Run around the woods like a bear.

VATZLAV. Nothing else?

MR BAT. ... and roar from time to time ...

VATZLAV. That's easy.

MR BAT. To frighten the flocks.

VATZLAV. Leave it to me. They won't have a minute's peace. Is that all?

MR BAT. That's all. (*He takes a coin from his pocket.*) Here's an advance.

VATZLAV (*examining the coin*). What? Only one? For such a difficult animal?

MR BAT. You'll get the balance later.

VATZLAV (*putting the coin in his pocket*). Okay, its a deal. By the sweat of thy brow.

MR BAT. But remember, no talking. You're an animal now and dumb's the word. Forget that you understand what people say. Forget you have a tongue.

VATZLAV (*sticking out his tongue*). Ahhh ...
MR BAT. Put it away and shut up. (*To* MRS BAT) Now
　　we have a bear.
　　　　(*They go out left.*)

SCENE 5

VATZLAV (*sticking out his tongue at them*). Ah ... 'Now
　　we have a bear.' Hear that, Daddy? Never thought
　　I'd sink so low, did you? But it might have been
　　worse. (*Boastfully*) I'm lord of the forest, all the
　　other animals are my vassals. And now let's visit
　　our kingdom. Forest, watch your step, here comes
　　your master. (*He goes out left.*)

SCENE 6

Enter from the right BOBBIE, *a sturdy man in his
forties. He is wearing a little boy's sailor suit that is
much too tight for him. Blue blouse with a wide collar.
Short blue trousers, white knee socks, black shoes. He
is holding a hoop and stick. He has a ring on his finger.
Around his neck a chain to which a gold watch is
attached.*

BOBBIE. Oh, when will Daddy and Mummy get back. I don't like it when they go off by themselves. I dreamt about Daddy last night. He was holding a fork in one hand and a knife in the other. Then Mummy came in with a frying pan. Daddy sharpened the knife on the fork and Mummy rubbed me with butter. They put me in the frying pan. 'Daddy,' I asked, 'is it a surprise?' And Daddy said: 'It needs marjoram.' 'Daddy,' I asked, 'why marjoram?' 'You're too young, you'll understand later on.' And before I could say Jack Robinson I was seasoned. With marjoram and other herbs. 'Look,' says Mummy, 'He's getting all red.' 'Splendid,' says Daddy, 'he tastes best when he's red.'

SCENE 7

Enter from the right MR *and* MRS BAT.

BOBBIE. Oh, Mummy, Mummy! (*He hugs* MRS BAT.)
MR BAT. Why are you so red?
MRS BAT (*putting her hand on* BOBBIE'*s forehead*). Your little face is on fire.
MR BAT (*aside*). Red in my house?
MRS BAT. How pink you are …
BOBBIE. Pink?
MRS BAT. As a red rose.
MR BAT (*aside*). Oh! A rose!

BOBBIE. It's because I'm so glad to see you both again. (*Aside*) Oh my goodness, I've told a lie.

MR BAT. We're glad too. (*Aside*) Those ruddy cheeks arouse my desires. But heavens, he's my son. Oh, if he were only green.

MRS BAT. That flesh-and-blood colour is so becoming to you ...

MR BAT. Stop!

BOBBIE. It's becoming to you too, Mummy.

MRS BAT. Silly boy, I'm always so pale.

BOBBIE. But now you're blushing.

MRS BAT. That's odd.

BOBBIE. If I'm like a rose, you're like ...

MR BAT. Stop!

MRS BAT. What's the matter?

BOBBIE. Daddy's as white as a sheet.

MR BAT. I'm thirsty.

BOBBIE. I'll get you some water.

MR BAT. Water. Ha ha!

BOBBIE. A glass of wine.

MR BAT. Wine. Ha ha!

BOBBIE. Or some sherbet ...

MR BAT. Sherbet. Ha ha! I want ... raspberries!

BOBBIE. I'll go get raspberries.

MR BAT. Don't put yourself out.

BOBBIE. I'll tell the butler to bring you a whole bowl of them.

MR BAT. They've got to be fresh.

BOBBIE. I'll go to the woods.

MR BAT. You stay here. We'll go.

BOBBIE. I'll go with you.

MR BAT. No, we wish to be by ourselves.

BOBBIE. Always by yourselves.

MR BAT. Goodbye.

(MR *and* MRS BAT *go out left*.)

MR BAT (*off*). Raspberries! Raspberries!

SCENE 8

BOBBIE. Mummy and Daddy have a secret. They're hiding something. Who are they hiding it from? From me. Who am I? A child. So it must be a secret that's not for children. It must be a sin. What! Can it be that my parents are sinners? But it's sinful of me to think such thoughts. I'd better stop or I won't be a good child any more. But if my parents are sinners, how *can* I be a good child? On the other hand, I could be the wicked child of good parents. Or worse: I could be the good child of wicked parents. In the first case I should be wronging them, in the second they would be wronging me. Either way, you'd have injustice. Only a good child of good parents or a wicked child of wicked parents can meet the requirements of justice.

MR BAT (*off*). Raspberries! Raspberries!

BOBBIE. What can they be doing in the woods? I'll follow them! (*He goes out left*.)

24

SCENE 9

Enter from the right VATZLAV *wearing the bear mask.*

VATZLAV. Whew! ... Why did I let myself in for this bear business? You run yourself ragged. I wouldn't wish it on my worst enemy. A shoemaker or a tailor can sit by the fire and nobody finds fault with their work. Suppose I sat by the fire! Oh no, a bear's got to roam the woods. Who ever saw a bear outside of the woods?

A VOICE (*off*). Me.

VATZLAV. Ho! Who dares to contradict me, the king of the forest?

SCENE 10

Enter from the left QUAIL, *the peasant.*

QUAIL. Your humble servant.

VATZLAV. Poor devil, come closer. Do you know whom you're addressing?

QUAIL. Sure thing. His lordship the bear.

VATZLAV. Well spoken.

QUAIL. His worship the bear.

25

VATZLAV. You seem to be an intelligent animal. Who are you?

QUAIL. Quail.

VATZLAV. A low-class bird. A quail can't hold a candle to a bear.

QUAIL. I'm not a bird. I'm a man.

VATZLAV. Are you sure?

QUAIL. Sure as shit.

VATZLAV. A quail man?

QUAIL. Quail's my name. It runs in the family.

VATZLAV. That doesn't prove anything. What do you do for a living?

QUAIL. I work in the boss man's fields.

VATZLAV. Hm. A peasant. Never mind. The noble bear deigns to talk to the humble peasant. See here, Quail. Did you say you'd seen a bear outside the woods?

QUAIL. Well, not exactly. I've seen his skin, though.

VATZLAV. Is that a joke?

QUAIL. It's a funny thing about a bear and his skin. He's not always in it. Sometimes, you see, the skin's in one place and the bear's someplace else.

VATZLAV. Do they hunt much around here?

QUAIL. Yep. When there's game.

VATZLAV. Quail, dear Mr Quail, take me with you.

QUAIL. God forbid. Your place is in the boss man's woods. I'd be in a fine fix if the warden found your skin in my hut. They're hard on poachers in these parts.

VATZLAV. That's not what I meant. I'll work for you,
    I'll milk your cows ...
QUAIL. Oh, no.
VATZLAV. ... mind the children, chop wood ...
QUAIL. Can't be did. You belong to the boss.
VATZLAV. Tell me this at least : is he a hard master?
QUAIL. He's easier on bears than on people. (*Goes out
    left.*)

SCENE 11

VATZLAV (*takes off his mask*). So it could be worse. But
    it's pretty bad all the same. When there's game,
    they hunt. Better to be a slave than to lose my skin
    in freedom. Maybe prison isn't so bad. You keep
    warm, they let you breathe, even if the stench
    turns your stomach. Did a man ever die of disgust?
    No. But plenty of men have died because they
    were disgusted with disgust. Serves them right,
    that's the sin of pride, thinking you're better than
    the other people. 'Maybe this is all right for other
    people, but I personally can't stand it.' That's what
    they say. God gave all men a nose to smell with,
    so why rebel against equality? Where do you find
    more equality than in prison? If we're all equal
    by nature, nature must want us to be in prison
    and not free. Morality, too, because you can starve

in freedom, and in prison they always fed me. I'm beginning to think I didn't really appreciate prison. A peaceful life, a secure old age – that's what I gave up. The hunters will come and kill me. What good is freedom when you're not the hunter but the hunted? Down with the hunters! Long live the bears!

SCENE 12

Enter from right MR *and* MRS BAT.

MR BAT. What's that again?

VATZLAV (*putting the mask back on*). Long live the hunters!

MR BAT. Your orders were to be silent. Why are you shouting?

VATZLAV. Oh, master, I was thinking what a beautiful thing the hunt is. Ah, the hunt. The horns, the hounds ...

MR BAT. You're to keep still. See?

VATZLAV. But I can't. The sound of horns in the early morning, the joyous cries of the beaters – the thought of it filled me with such delight, such love for the hunters, even for the hounds, I couldn't help shouting ...

MR BAT. That'll do.

VATZLAV. Long live the hunt!

MR BAT. Silence!

VATZLAV. I will be silent, but the rapture of my heart cannot be stilled. No one can prevent me from loving in secret. Oh, hunters, how long must I wait for you?

(MR and MRS BAT go out left.)

SCENE 13

VATZLAV (taking off his mask). Maybe I overdid it. What if they unleash the pack? Here they come. No, it's a child.

SCENE 14

Enter BOBBIE from the right.

BOBBIE. So here I am in the forest. I can't see three steps ahead of me. But I won't turn back. Here I don't know what's in store for me, at home I know everything. And when you know everything, there's no hope.

VATZLAV. He looks flabby and stupid.

BOBBIE. O forest, forest, you've given me hope.

VATZLAV. I'll bet he's a coward.

BOBBIE. A hope of hope.

VATZLAV. I'll scare him out of his wits. Good God! That's the only pleasure I have left! (*He puts on the mask, bounds in front of* BOBBIE *and roars.*)

BOBBIE. Why are you roaring?

(VATZLAV *roars louder.*)

Are you in pain?

(VATZLAV *roars very loud.*)

Don't you feel well?

VATZLAV (*taking off his mask*). You little snotnose, can't you see I'm a bear?

BOBBIE. Really? That's too bad. Then go ahead and roar.

VATZLAV. Aren't you afraid?

BOBBIE. Not at all.

VATZLAV. But look here, I'm a wild beast. Why aren't you afraid?

BOBBIE. That's just it. I know who you are and when I know something, it doesn't frighten me.

VATZLAV. But suppose I ate you up?

BOBBIE. Then I'd be eaten. I'd be even less frightened than now.

VATZLAV. You lack experience. I remember a time when even the dead were afraid because they didn't know whether they were dead or still alive. My father begot me in fear, my mother bore me in dread. The moment I was born, I tried to turn back, I knocked at her womb and begged her to let me in. But she wouldn't take me back, because there's a severe penalty for harbouring guilty persons. Sometimes, when I was a baby, I sucked a sword instead of my mother's breast, and then when she gave me her breast I was afraid, I thought it was a sword. They sent me to school and I graduated with the degree of Doctor of Fear. And now I'll give you a piece of advice: be afraid, little rosebud, be afraid.

BOBBIE. No, my dear sir, I'm not afraid of you.

VATZLAV. Ah, woe is me!

BOBBIE. You've had an unhappy childhood, I agree. Try not to think of it.

VATZLAV. Oh, wretched fate!

BOBBIE. You were unhappy, but now cheer up.

VATZLAV. Oh, misery, misery!

BOBBIE. Let's be friends. Put it there.

VATZLAV. Oh, have pity!

BOBBIE. Forget the past.

VATZLAV. Forget the past? Those glorious days? No one was ever beaten like me. Understand? No one. I hold the world's record for beatings received, and I'm proud of it. You can search the whole earth and you won't find anyone who can boast such beatings. No one can take away the glory of my martyrdom. If anyone tells me he was beaten, I will answer that I was beaten more.

BOBBIE. I see. You want to build a monument to your degradation.

VATZLAV. Down on your knees to it.

BOBBIE. To make a virtue of your weakness.

VATZLAV. Pray to it.

BOBBIE. To find beauty in your humiliation.

VATZLAV. Why shouldn't I?

BOBBIE. I don't see what you're complaining about. I believe you were made to walk on all fours. With all the pleasure you seem to get out of your misery, what more do you need to make you happy?

VATZLAV. I want to be feared. Is it fair that I should be afraid of everyone and that no one should be afraid of me? No, it's not fair. There will be no justice in the world until I've scared someone shitless. Can't you think of someone?

BOBBIE. You mean somebody weaker than you?

VATZLAV. That's right.

BOBBIE. No, I'm afraid not.

VATZLAV. Not for my personal benefit, it's for the principle.

BOBBIE. Oh, if it's for the principle, cheer up. We'll find somebody.

VATZLAV. I like you, son. We foreigners are tender-hearted. We like to chat, to exchange ideas. We're not stones like the curious specimens around here, who'd rather die than open their mouths. We may be uncouth, but at least we're sincere. Warm-hearted folk who speak our minds …

BOBBIE. Tell me, have you seen a child's parents around here?

VATZLAV. Honest, kindly …

BOBBIE. Still patting himself on the back.

VATZLAV. Simple, friendly …

BOBBIE. I asked you a question.

VATZLAV. Come to my arms. (*He embraces* BOBBIE.) I'm so moved.

BOBBIE. Aren't you ever going to answer me?

VATZLAV. Brother, I love you.

BOBBIE. Then you've seen them?

VATZLAV. If the old skinflint and exploiter of bears is your father, I saw him going that way with his wife.

BOBBIE. Take me to them.

(*They go out left.*)

SCENE 15

Enter from right the peasants QUAIL *and* SASSAFRAS.

SASSAFRAS. They say something's going to happen.

QUAIL. You think ... psst ... psst ...

SASSAFRAS. Sh ... Sh ...

QUAIL. I haven't said a word.

SASSAFRAS. You haven't said a word, but you've said it mighty loud.

QUAIL. Scarecat!

SASSAFRAS. I'm no scarecat, but I keep my bravery to myself.

QUAIL. It seems they've seen a comet.

SASSAFRAS. Heavenly saints.

QUAIL. With a long tail.

SASSAFRAS. That looks like …

QUAIL. Sh … Sh …

SASSAFRAS. I haven't said a word.

QUAIL. But you were going to.

SASSAFRAS. All right. No tail.

QUAIL. Why no tail?

SASSAFRAS. Don't contradict me, neighbour. (*Raising his voice.*) No tail!

QUAIL. All right, all right.

SASSAFRAS (*under his breath*). Well, what about that tail?

(QUAIL *whispers in his ear.*)

I don't believe it.

QUAIL. As true as I'm standing here.

SASSAFRAS. What do you think of that?

MR BAT (*off*). Raspberries! Raspberries!

QUAIL. Of what, neighbour?

SASSAFRAS. I haven't said a word.

QUAIL. I thought you did.

SASSAFRAS. You think too much.

QUAIL. So do you.

(SASSAFRAS *and* QUAIL *go out left.*)

SCENE 16

Enter from right VATZLAV *and* BOBBIE.

VATZLAV. I'm telling you, friend, everybody loves me,
the women most of all. The way they ran after me,
I couldn't get rid of them. Some days, I remember,
I used to shut myself up in the house, just to be
alone. I'm reading my paper and whistling – I'm
musical, you see. When all of a sudden, bam! A
dame flies in through the window. The poor thing
was so crazy about me she jumped right in with
her eyes closed. Trouble, trouble. Cost me a fortune
in windowpanes alone. The glaziers all knew me.
When they passed me on the street, they'd say:
'At your service, sir, any windowpanes today?'
BOBBIE. Climb a tree and report.
(VATZLAV *climbs on* BOBBIE'S *shoulders.*)
BOBBIE. What do you see?
VATZLAV. People.
BOBBIE. What kind of people?
VATZLAV. Scum.
BOBBIE. Just plain people?
VATZLAV. Oh, oh no. There's my boss and his wife.
BOBBIE. Let me up. (BOBBIE *climbs on* VATZLAV'S *shoul-
ders.*) Good God, what is he doing? All tangled up
with the people. Feasting on the people?
VATZLAV. You'll find out.
BOBBIE. On the body of the people. His suckers are
clinging to the body of the people, he's strangling

them with his awful tentacles ... Oh Father, oh my
father ...

VATZLAV. What about your father?

BOBBIE. He's drinking the blood of the people!

VATZLAV. Nice daddy you've got there. Congratulations.

CHORUS OF THE PEOPLE (off). Drink our blood, my
lord!

VOICE OF A WOMAN OF THE PEOPLE (off). I've got a baby
here, a luscious baby. Help yourself, my lord!

CHORUS (off). Drink up, my lord!

VOICE OF A MAN OF THE PEOPLE (off). I'm an old man
bowed with age, bled since childhood, but there's
still some left.

CHORUS (off). Drink up, my lord!

VOICE OF MAN OF THE PEOPLE (off). We haven't got
many red corpuscles left, but you're welcome ...

VOICE OF WOMAN OF THE PEOPLE (off). We beg you ...

CHORUS (off). Drink our blood, my lord!

BOBBIE. Oh, Father, Father, so that's your raspberries.
You never told me about your loathsome meals,
your lunches, your dinners, your snacks ...

VATZLAV. It wasn't anything to brag about.

BOBBIE. Maybe breakfast, too.

VATZLAV. Very likely.

BOBBIE. You talked about raspberries and you drank
the blood of the people.

VATZLAV. There you have it.

BOBBIE. My father! A bloodsucker!

(*They exit right,* BOBBIE *on* VATZLAV'S *shoulders.*)

SCENE 17

Enter SASSAFRAS *and* QUAIL *from left.*

QUAIL. Did they suck your blood, neighbour?

SASSAFRAS. Sure did.

QUAIL. The boss sucked me dry.

SASSAFRAS. The boss is nothing. The missus is worse.
When she gets her suckers into you, heaven help
you.

QUAIL. Oh well, it's all in the day's work.

SASSAFRAS. They say Jake saw Justice.

QUAIL. Where'd he see her?

SASSAFRAS. Swimming in the pond over near Gloomy
Glen.

QUAIL. Naked?

SASSAFRAS. Sure thing. Pretty too.

QUAIL. You know what, neighbour? S'pose we go over
Gloomy Glen way.

SASSAFRAS. Take a look at Justice?

QUAIL. Leastways not frogs.

SASSAFRAS. You in a hurry, neighbour?

QUAIL. If Jake can see her, why can't I?
(*They go out right.*)

SCENE 18

Enter from right VATZLAV *and* BOBBIE.

BOBBIE (*climbing down from* VATZLAV's *shoulders*). I don't want to be Mr Bat's little boy any more.

VATZLAV. What do you want to be?

BOBBIE. A bear.

VATZLAV. How you going to swing that?

BOBBIE. Let's swap. Give me your skin.

VATZLAV. What? Deny my shaggy parents? My dear old dad with his black nose and my four-footed mother? You've come to the wrong address.

BOBBIE. Dear quadruped, give me your parentage.

VATZLAV. I love them so.

BOBBIE. Do it for me.

VATZLAV. Let me think. Only an unworthy son renounces his parents. But an unworthy son never renounces his parents for nothing, that would be bad business. I can't let you have them for nothing, because only an unworthy son renounces his parents and if I let you have them for nothing I wouldn't be an unworthy son. You follow me?

BOBBIE. I'll give you my watch. (*He gives* VATZLAV *his watch.*)

VATZLAV. That's different. I'm turning into an unworthy son, I can feel it.

BOBBIE. Will that do it?

VATZLAV. I'm not a hundred per cent unworthy yet.

38

BOBBIE. Take my ring. (*He gives* VATZLAV *his ring.*)

VATZLAV. That's for daddy. What do I get for mummy?

BOBBIE. I haven't got anything else.

VATZLAV. Oh well. Let's say I've sold all of daddy and only part of mummy. Maybe it's better that way. I'm not renouncing my family entirely. (*He gives* BOBBIE *his mask.*) Goodbye, bear. (*He goes out right.*)

BOBBIE (*putting on the mask*). Goodbye, Bat family! (*He goes out left.*)

SCENE 19

Enter on the right the GENIUS. *Antique morning-coat, bushy black beard. He is bald* JUSTINE *runs in from the left. She is a beautiful girl in a white muslin dress; on her head a wreath of daisies.*

JUSTINE (*presses her head against the* GENIUS'S *chest*). Oh Father, Father!

THE GENIUS. What's the matter, child?

JUSTINE. I went to the meadow to plait a wreath.

THE GENIUS. No harm in that. It's most becoming.

JUSTINE. When I'd finished, I looked at my reflection in the pond.

THE GENIUS. All perfectly innocent so far.

39

JUSTINE. While I was looking at myself, a peasant came out of the bushes and gaped at me.

THE GENIUS. You can't forbid an honest peasant to look at you.

JUSTINE. But he wasn't honest.

THE GENIUS. Mustn't say that. Only the rich are dishonest, the poor are always honest.

JUSTINE. This one wasn't.

THE GENIUS. How do you know?

JUSTINE. Because when I took off my dress ...

THE GENIUS. Oh, you took off your dress?

JUSTINE. I was going to bathe.

THE GENIUS. And then?

JUSTINE. He took out a stick and threatened me.

THE GENIUS. With a stick?

JUSTINE. Or something like it.

THE GENIUS. And then?

JUSTINE. I thought he was going to hit me, so I ran away. I hardly had time to pick up my dress.

THE GENIUS. That was naughty of you.

JUSTINE. Should I have let him hurt me?

THE GENIUS. He had no intention of hurting you.

JUSTINE. He was shaking that cruel instrument ...

THE GENIUS. Because he was feeling happy.

JUSTINE. Swinging it in all directions ...

THE GENIUS. Suppose he was. It's only human that when a poor devil is feeling happy and has something in his hand he shakes it.

JUSTINE. Then he wasn't going to hurt me?

THE GENIUS. Of course not.

40

JUSTINE. But I thought …

THE GENIUS. You mustn't have such thoughts, my dear.

JUSTINE. Where do babies come from?

THE GENIUS. What did you say?

JUSTINE. I'm a big girl now and I ought to know.

THE GENIUS. You're right, child. Well … babies … from the head.

JUSTINE. Really?

THE GENIUS. By the working of reason. The same as in nature. Look at the flowers, the little birds … Nature is reasonable.

JUSTINE. You're making fun of my innocence.

THE GENIUS. I begot you with my head …

JUSTINE (*momentarily shocked*). Oh, Daddy!

THE GENIUS. And bore you with my head. Or better still, with my reason. I am at once your father and mother.

JUSTINE. I've had no experience in these things, but I don't see how … With the head, by the head … Is it hard to do?

THE GENIUS. It all depends. Not for me, because I'm a genius, the inspired leader of mankind.

JUSTINE. Of course. There's no one as wise as you, Father … or should I say Mother?

THE GENIUS. As you wish.

JUSTINE. I suppose I'll have to believe you. And since you're the wisest of men, you must have created me for some purpose. Why did you bring me into the world?

THE GENIUS. A pertinent question. I'm glad to find you

41

so reasonable. It proves that you really are my daughter. Know then that injustice governs the world.

JUSTINE. What does that mean?

THE GENIUS. Some are rich, others are poor.

JUSTINE. What has that got to do with me?

THE GENIUS. Patience! We know that everything in the world has its contrary. Consequently, if injustice exists, justice must also exist.

JUSTINE. That sounds reasonable. But does it?

THE GENIUS. No.

JUSTINE. What a shame!

THE GENIUS. But justice must exist.

JUSTINE. You just said it didn't.

THE GENIUS. Have you forgotten reason? Thanks to reason, my child, everything can be set right, for the world is reasonable. Since justice does not exist, it must be invented. And that's why I created you, the fruit of necessity fertilized by reason.

SCENE 20

VATZLAV *enters from the right. Bobbie's ring is on his finger and he wears Bobbie's watch on a chain around his neck. He eavesdrops on the conversation.*

THE GENIUS. You are Justice.

JUSTINE. And what am I supposed to do?

THE GENIUS. Exactly what you've been doing. Bathe in the pond, take your hair down at night and braid it in the morning.

JUSTINE. That's easy.

THE GENIUS. And when a poor peasant wants to look at you, let him look.

JUSTINE. His eyes were so strange ...

THE GENIUS. And don't swaddle yourself in superfluous clothing.

JUSTINE. I always take my clothes off to bathe.

THE GENIUS. Take them off even when you're not going to bathe.

JUSTINE. Really? What for?

THE GENIUS. How shall I put it ... You are Justice, the sight of you arouses a noble desire for justice. Inflamed by this desire, the poor will turn against the rich and do great things. They will build a new order, and in that new order you will be queen.

JUSTINE. Queen? Oh, I'd like that.

THE GENIUS. Therefore show yourself to the people.

JUSTINE. Oh, I will. I will.

THE GENIUS. Let them see you in all your beauty.

JUSTINE. Yes! Yes!

THE GENIUS. Up until now Mr Bat has held the stage with his ugliness. Now your beauty will take over.

(JUSTINE *starts to undress.*)

No! Don't fling off your clothes like a farm girl. Disrobe with circumspection, hesitate, so making it clear that you are undressing, not for the audience, but for yourself. Make some show of reluctance, as though fighting down your shame; let your secret lewdness gain the upper hand, but very slowly. Your lewdness will be measured by the shame you overcome. Begin discreetly, unveil a little, then a little more. Stop from time to time. They'll think your reluctance is winning out, but all the while they'll be certain of the contrary. For remember this: Certainty is the strongest of lures.

JUSTINE. Don't worry. I'll drive them mad, they'll follow me to the end of the world.

THE GENIUS. Your frivolities will serve the cause. Meanwhile I shall go abroad to gain allies. I shall proclaim your name to many peoples and they will join ranks with us. Await my return. Farewell, my daughter. (*He goes out right.*)

JUSTINE. Goodbye, Father. (*She goes out left.*)

44

SCENE 21

VATZLAV. Justice? I've heard of her, but this is the first time I've seen her face to face. Well, let's see what's in it for me. (*He goes out left.*)

SCENE 22

Enter from the right SASSAFRAS *and* QUAIL.

QUAIL. Say, where is this Gloomy Glen?

SASSAFRAS. It can't be far.

QUAIL. How do you know?

SASSAFRAS. 'Cause if it's far, we've taken the wrong path.

QUAIL. You know what, neighbour Sassafras? Something tells me that if it's the wrong path we ought to turn around.

SASSAFRAS. Think so?

QUAIL. Why should we go the wrong way?

SASSAFRAS. All right, we'll turn around. (*They do so.*) Is it still far?

QUAIL. It all depends. If we're going the right way now, it can't be far. If we're not, contrariwise.

SASSAFRAS. You know what, neighbour Quail? Somethings tells me we ought to turn around.

QUAIL. What makes you think that?

SASSAFRAS. 'Cause if one direction is wrong, the other must be right.

QUAIL. You got something there. (*They turn around again.*) Neighbour.

SASSAFRAS. What?

QUAIL. Supposing the other's right and this one's wrong?

SASSAFRAS. Holy mackerel!

QUAIL. I'll tell you what, Sassafras. Let's go arm in arm.

SASSAFRAS. What for?

QUAIL. 'Cause supposing I was going the wrong way and you were going the right way, you'd lead me the right way. And supposing I was going the right way and you were going the wrong way, I'd hold you back.

SASSAFRAS. Good idea. (*They go arm in arm.*)

QUAIL. This way.

SASSAFRAS. No, that way.

QUAIL. Neighbour, seems to me you're going wrong.

SASSAFRAS. It seems to me you're going wrong.

QUAIL. I'm right and you're wrong.

SASSAFRAS. You must be blind.

QUAIL. Who's blind?

SASSAFRAS. You.

QUAIL. Then you're a chipmunk.

SASSAFRAS. A chipmunk?

QUAIL. Well, if you're not a chipmunk, you're a donkey.

SASSAFRAS. What's that again?

QUAIL. I say you're stupid, neighbour.

SASSAFRAS. And you're a baboon.

QUAIL. What?

SASSAFRAS. You heard me.

QUAIL (*imitates the braying of an ass*). Hee-haw, hee-haw!

> (*They rush at each other and fight.*)

SCENE 23

Enter right BOBBIE *with the bear mask on his face and carrying writing materials.*

BOBBIE. Have you seen the boss man's son?

SASSAFRAS. I've seen a baboon! (*He beats* QUAIL.)

QUAIL. I've seen an ass! (*He beats* SASSAFRAS.)

BOBBIE. They haven't seen me. That's fine. It proves my disguise is effective and that no one recognizes me. This is a new life. Oh, how beautiful it is to begin a new life, to strip off the past. It's true I haven't had much of a past, but what there was of it was so degrading – Oh, there seems to be some disagreement between you two. What are you fighting about?

SASSAFRAS *and* QUAIL (*in unison*). Justice.

BOBBIE. An excellent cause. Justice is worthy of every sacrifice. But why should you be fighting?

QUAIL (*hitting* SASSAFRAS). Because he's a donkey.

BOBBIE. I infer that you yourself are not a donkey, because members of the same family don't fight among themselves. That's why I've become a bear, so I could fight the Bats. Who are you?

SASSAFRAS (*hitting* QUAIL). Baboon!

BOBBIE. Are you hitting him because he's a baboon or because you're a donkey?

QUAIL. Hear that? Answer the gentleman, you donkey.

SASSAFRAS. I'm hitting him because I'm not a donkey.

BOBBIE. That's odd. I could see the point if you *were* a donkey.

    (QUAIL *gets the upper hand, sits down on* SASSAFRAS *and thrashes him.*)

What about you? Why are you hitting him?

QUAIL. Because I'm not a baboon.

BOBBIE. Then maybe you're a donkey and he's a baboon? Speak up. Let's get to the bottom of this.

QUAIL. No, he's the donkey.

BOBBIE. Then you must be the baboon.

SASSAFRAS. See? What did I tell you?

QUAIL. I'm Quail.

SASSAFRAS. And I'm Sassafras. (*They stop fighting.*)

BOBBIE. Then where are the animals you were talking about just now? – Never mind. Weren't you headed for a certain place where Justice is said to have appeared?

QUAIL *and* SASSAFRAS (*in unison*). Yes, sir.

BOBBIE. Then my advice to you is to get going. Don't waste your time arguing about who's a donkey and who's a baboon. Leave that to the bear, who has his own opinion. Make haste, because I'm confident that when you poor yokels reach your destination, your lives will be changed. Justice will make men of you even if what Sassafras says of Quail and Quail says of Sassafras is true.

QUAIL. What do you think, neighbour?

SASSAFRAS. That's no ordinary bear. He's educated.

QUAIL. Yeah.

SASSAFRAS. He talks like a minister.

QUAIL. Yeah, he ain't the same. He wasn't so smart when I saw him the other day.

SASSAFRAS. Maybe he's been going to school.

(SASSAFRAS *and* QUAIL *go out left.*)

SCENE 24

Enter VATZLAV *from the right.*

VATZLAV (*seeing* BOBBIE-THE-BEAR). Oooh! (*Runs out left.*)

BOBBIE. Wait!

VATZLAV. I'm not so dumb.

BOBBIE (*removing his mask*). Don't you know your old friend?

49

VATZLAV. Oh, it's you. Thank God. I thought it was me.

BOBBIE. Are you afraid of yourself?

VATZLAV. You can't imagine how terrifying I am. I know myself.

BOBBIE. But you sold me your skin. Don't you remember?

VATZLAV. I've been so distraught.

BOBBIE. I can see that. What's wrong?

VATZLAV. Too much on my mind.

BOBBIE. What have you been doing with yourself?

VATZLAV. Not much. But I've got something cooking now. If it works out, I'll buy you a drink.

BOBBIE. Buy me one now.

VATZLAV. It's not in the bag yet.

BOBBIE. You're leaving?

VATZLAV. I'm in a hurry.

BOBBIE. I need you. Could you deliver a letter for me?

VATZLAV. I've got this deal …

BOBBIE. It won't run away.

VATZLAV. Business waits for no man. Be good. (*He goes out left.*)

SCENE 25

BOBBIE (*puts his mask on and writes*). 'Dear Mummy
    ...' No, not mummy. I'm a bear now, she's not
    my mother any more. 'Dear Madam. The writer of
    this letter was your son, but he was devoured by
    a bear. I am no longer your son, I am a wild, free
    and independent bear. If you wish to see me, I shall
    be in the forest waiting for you. Your bear.'
A VOICE (*off*). I watch. I watch.
BOBBIE. That's my father's flunkey and spy. Luckily
    he's blind. Yoo-hoo! Here I am!

SCENE 26

Enter from the right OEDIPUS, *curly beard, Greek
robe, blind-man's white cane.*

OEDIPUS (*groping around with his cane*). Where?
BOBBIE (*taking* OEDIPUS *by the hand*). Here.
OEDIPUS. What are you doing?
BOBBIE. Writing a letter.
OEDIPUS. To whom?
BOBBIE. My mother.
OEDIPUS. Let me read it. (*He takes the letter and turns*

51

it in all directions.) I don't see very well. Read it to me.

BOBBIE (*takes the letter and reads*). 'Dear Madam, wife of my beloved father. I regret to inform you that I love him much more than I love you. Kindly assure him of my profound respect and affection. I belong to him alone. His obedient servant and son.'

OEDIPUS. I will deliver it.

BOBBIE. I hate to inconvenience you.

OEDIPUS. Give me that letter at once.

BOBBIE. As you wish.

OEDIPUS. I watch. I watch. (*He goes out right with letter.*)

SCENE 27

BOBBIE. Now he's sure to deliver my letter. (*He goes out left.*)

SCENE 28

Enter right MRS BAT, *with a rose in her corsage. She is holding a fan. She is drawing a meticulously clipped black poodle by a string. The poodle is a dummy on*

wheels. On his neck a silver bell and a red bow. Little
red bows on his paws and tail. On his head a red cap.

MRS BAT. Little sweetums. Pretty Doggy-woggy. Tell
me, little sweetums, do you love your mistress?
Do you care for her a teensy-weensy bit? No, little
sweetums doesn't love her. Naughty, naughty,
naughty. I'm angry with Doggy-woggy. Bad, bad,
horrid Doggy-woggy. Your mistress is angry. She's
going to leave you. (*She goes to one side.*) Is
Doggy-woggy sad now? That's what he gets for
not loving his mistress. It's all his fault. Ohhh. Is
little sweetums crying? (*She comes back to him.*)
Don't be sad, your mistress forgives you. Look,
she's right here. Please don't cry, you'll break her
heart. Oh, do please stop, it was all in fun. Come,
little sweetums, come to Mummy. (*She rocks him
in her arms.*) Good little Doggy-woggy. Mummy
loves her good little dear little Doggy-woggy. Here,
let me tickle you to make you laugh. Now what?
Oh, you fresh thing! (*She puts the dog down.*) Now
listen to me, you belong to Mummy and you've got
to do what she says. Come here! (*She pulls the
dog to her and puts the fan in its mouth.*) Sit up!
(*She threatens him with her finger.*) You do as I
say or it's all over between us. Did you think I'd
let you get away with such insolence? (*She stamps
her foot.*) So Doggy thought he could get fresh
with Mummy. (*Pause. She pets him.*) Nice little
Doggy-woggy. Good little Doggy-woggy. Cunning

53

little Doggy-woggy. (*Losing patience*) So pretty! So well-behaved! (*In anger*) Oh! Oh! So well-behaved. (*She screams.*) WHY ARE YOU SO WELL-BEHAVED? (*She bursts into tears.*) Always the same, always the same ... Obedient, polite, cunning. It's driving me crazy ... (*Furious*) Why don't you say something? (*Bellows.*) Stupid dog, why don't you say something?

SCENE 29

Enter right OEDIPUS *with the letter.*

OEDIPUS. Where are you, madam?

MRS BAT. I'm not here.

OEDIPUS. I have a letter for you.

MRS BAT. Here I am! (*She takes the letter and reads it.*) Heavens!

OEDIPUS. Yes, madam. Yes, yes. That's how it is. Now what do you think ... I can't hear you, madam.

MRS BAT (*to herself*). A bear?

OEDIPUS. Who?

MRS BAT. Nobody. (*She goes out left, pulling Doggy-woggy.*)

SCENE 30

OEDIPUS. What bear? (*He goes out right.*)

SCENE 31

Enter SASSAFRAS *and* QUAIL *from the right.*

QUAIL (*limping*). If this goes on, neighbour, Justice can lick my ass. I got a blister on my left heel and I can feel one coming on my right heel if we don't find her pretty soon.

SCENE 32

Enter VATZLAV *from the left. Over his shirt a loud yellow blazer with silver trimming, in glaring contrast to his shirt, ragged trousers, and the great clodhoppers he is wearing. Bowler hat. On his finger the ring, around his neck the watch.*

VATZLAV. Well, gentlemen, you've come to the right place.

QUAIL. Gentlemen? Does he mean us?

SASSAFRAS. Must be some mistake.

VATZLAV. No mistake. The customer's always right and that makes him a gentleman.

QUAIL. You're very kind, sir ... Who are you?

VATZLAV (*bowing*). An artist.

QUAIL. Then you're a kind artist. But we're looking for a certain person that Jake saw by the pond in Gloomy Glen. Have you seen her?

VATZLAV. She's right here. Be seated, gentlemen.

QUAIL. Do you see her, Sassafras?

SASSAFRAS (*with dignity*). *Mister* Sassafras.

QUAIL. I don't see a thing. Let us pass, sir. We got no time to lose.

VATZLAV. There she is. (*He points left.*)

    (SASSAFRAS *moves to the left.*)

QUAIL. Hiding right here? Who'd have thought it? God bless you, sir ... Hey, where you going, neighbour Sassafras?

SASSAFRAS (*with dignity*). *Mister* Sassafras.

QUAIL (*barring the way*). Let me go first.

SASSAFRAS (*haughtily*). Beg your pardon, Quail. I go first.

QUAIL. I go first. (*They jostle each other.*)

VATZLAV. Don't push, gentlemen. Pay your money and there'll be room for everybody.

QUAIL. Money? Jake saw her for free.

VATZLAV. Because if you pay, we all stand to gain; if it's free nobody gains but you. And Justice means equal gain for all. Don't be unjust when you're looking for Justice.

SASSAFRAS. She was supposed to be in Gloomy Glen, down by the pond.

VATZLAV. Ah, rustic simplicity. Do you think Justice grows in the swamps like rushes, do you think she wades knee-deep in water like a heron? No, my simple-minded friends. Justice is a product not of nature but of reason. She is a delicate creature prone to pneumonia. And just for your convenience you want her to appear under the open sky, in the wind and rain, in ice and snow. And for nothing! You ought to be ashamed of yourselves. Goodbye.

QUAIL. Do we pay, neighbour?

SASSAFRAS. Maybe he'll give us a reduction.

VATZLAV. You still here?

QUAIL. He won't come down.

SASSAFRAS. All right, we'll pay. (*They take money from their pockets.*)

VATZLAV (*pocketing the money*). You're in luck. I'm giving you the last two seats.

(VATZLAV, SASSAFRAS *and* QUAIL *go out left.*)

SCENE 33

MRS BAT *enters from the left pulling Doggy-woggy, who has her fan in his mouth.*

MRS BAT. I dreamt I was going through the woods. Suddenly you jumped out of the bushes. Your jaws were wide open and you had terrible white fangs. I ran away and came to a clearing. In the clearing there was an enormous spit. My husband was turning it. He was wearing a chef's hat and he said, 'He's turned red. He tastes best when he's red.' And you were on the spit. I didn't want to eat you, but you came running after me. I'm lost, I thought, unless I can escape into my own belly. Then … (*She screams.*) How dare you suspect me! Take it back. You're nasty, disgusting, shameless. Do you realize what you're accusing me of? Is that what you've been thinking? At last I've had a glimpse of your sick brain. You vicious little choir-boy. How dare you be jealous of your own fiend-ish hallucinations? You've insulted me. That will do. Not another word. I won't listen to your rav-ings. I forbid you. Think what you please, but leave me out of it. I'm not talking to you. (*She turns her back on Doggy-woggy.*) Oh, no. Certainly not. (*After every sentence she pauses to listen to Doggy-woggy's answer.*) Really? – That's odd. – As you wish. – No. – No, I don't know him. – I've never laid eyes on him. – Ah, what's that?

What bear? – Well, what of it? – Do you want me to swear? – As you wish. – All right, I swear, now are you satisfied? – Starting in again? – I've just told you. – What more do you want to know? – I've told you everything. – That's enough. – I'm tired. – Oh, leave me alone. – Stop, stop. – I've had enough. – What *do* you want? – I refuse to answer. You bore me. – What? You've been spying on me? – You're vile, vile. You dared! – Serves you right. It's your own fault. – Yes, yes, yes, can I help it if you're not a bear?! – I love him! – Since when? From the very first moment. – No, go away. It's all over between us. – No, it's no use. – Ha ha! You, a bear? Don't even try. You're pathetic. – Don't beg me, don't apologize, you're wasting your time. – You won't? Then don't. (*She snatches her fan from the dog's mouth.*) I'm going away. (*She takes a few steps, drawing the dog behind her.*) Don't follow me. – You still here? – You threaten me? – Brute force? – Let me go. Take your paws off me! – Nothing can stop me! – I never want to see you again, understand? Nasty beast! (*She gives Doggy-woggy a kick and drops the leash.*) But don't forget the beauty of the fading rose. I'll leave you a memento. Be faithful to it. (*She takes the rose from her corsage and throws it to Doggy-woggy. She goes out right.*)

(*A moment later Doggy-woggy follows her slowly.*)

SCENE 34

A drum is heard. A little curtain drops from the flies.
VATZLAV *enters right beating the drum that is hang-*
ing from his neck. QUAIL *and* SASSAFRAS *follow.*

VATZLAV. Here we are. Be seated, gentlemen, be
seated. In a few moments Justice will appear.
> (QUAIL *and* SASSAFRAS *sit down side by side in*
> *front of the little curtain with their backs to the*
> *audience.*)
Anyone else? Anyone else? Golden opportunity.
Step in, step right in.

SCENE 35

Enter MR BAT *from the right.*

MR BAT. I want a seat in the orchestra.
VATZLAV (*running up eagerly*). Certainly, Your Excellency. For you we have the best place in the
house.
> (*He leads* MR BAT *towards the centre of the*
> *stage, gives* SASSAFRAS *and* QUAIL *a kick.*)
Hey, you, a seat for His Excellency.

(SASSAFRAS *and* QUAIL *go down on all fours side by side facing the audience.* VATZLAV *wipes their backs with his sleeve as though dusting a chair.*)

Here you are, Excellency. I think you'll be comfortable.

QUAIL. What about us?

(SASSAFRAS *puts his hand over* QUAIL's *mouth.* MR BAT *sits down on them facing the curtain, his back to the audience.*)

VATZLAV. Attention, please! (*He beats the drum, the curtain rises enough to show* JUSTINE *in the costume of a striptease artist.*) Men are born and always continue free and equal. Civil distinctions, therefore, can be founded only on public utility.

QUAIL. Can you see anything, neighbour Sassafras?

SASSAFRAS. Naw.

QUAIL. Me neither.

VATZLAV (*stops drumming*). What's that disturbance?

QUAIL. It ain't us, we're chairs.

VATZLAV. I beg your pardon, Excellency. That chair squeaks. (*He goes over to* QUAIL, *gives him a kick and returns to his place, beats the drum and goes on with his declamation, while* JUSTINE *undresses in the classical striptease style.*) The end of all political associations is the preservation of natural and imprescriptible rights of man; and these rights are liberty, property, security and resistance of oppression.

QUAIL. Say, man's got it good.

SASSAFRAS (*with a sigh*). Yeah, wouldn't you like to be him.

VATZLAV. Liberty consists in the power to do whatever does not injure another. The exercise of the natural rights of every man has no other limits than those which are necessary to secure to every other man the free exercise of the same rights.

QUAIL. Punch me in the jaw, neighbour.

SASSAFRAS. What for, neighbour?

QUAIL. So I can punch you back.

SASSAFRAS. Oh, that's different. (SASSAFRAS *punches* QUAIL. QUAIL *punches* SASSAFRAS.)

VATZLAV. The law ought to prohibit only actions hurtful to society. What is not prohibited by the law should not be hindered ...

(SASSAFRAS *sticks his finger up his nose.*)

QUAIL. Sassafras, take your finger out of your nose.

SASSAFRAS. It's my nose, ain't it? What harm does it do you?

QUAIL. It don't hurt me none but it looks bad.

SASSAFRAS. It's my right.

VATZLAV. And no man can be compelled to do what it does not expressly enjoin.

QUAIL. But nobody's making you.

SASSAFRAS. All right, I'll stop. (*He stops picking his nose.*)

VATZLAV. The law is an expression of the will of the community. All citizens have a right to concur, either personally or by their representatives, in its formation. It should be the same to all, whether it protects or punishes; and all being equal in its sight, are equally eligible for all honours, places and employments ... No man ought to be molested on account of his opinions, not even on account of his religious opinions, provided his avowal of them does not disturb the public order.

SASSAFRAS. Shit!

(VATZLAV *stops beating the drum.* JUSTINE *stops undressing.*)

VATZLAV (*severely*). Is that a thought or an opinion?

SASSAFRAS. We-ell ...

QUAIL. He don't really mean it.

VATZLAV (*beating the drum*). The unrestrained communication of thoughts and opinions being one of the most estimable rights of man, every citizen may speak, write and publish freely. (*He stops beating the drum. To* SASSAFRAS) So if it's a thought or an opinion you're expressing, that's all right. But if it's just plain shit ...

QUAIL. Which is it Sassafras?

SASSAFRAS. Shit.

VATZLAV (*to* QUAIL). Is he an anarchist?

QUAIL. Hell, no. He's wacky.

VATZLAV. We'll see about that. (*He beats the drum.* JUSTINE *goes on with her striptease.*) Every man being presumed innocent until he has been convicted, whenever his detention becomes indispensable, all rigour towards him, more than is necessary to secure his person, ought to be provided against by the law.

(JUSTINE *completes her striptease and takes her* *final pose.* MR BAT *applauds. The curtain falls,* *concealing* JUSTINE. VATZLAV *bows as if the* *applause were addressed to him.* MR BAT *goes* *out right.*)

SCENE 36

SASSAFRAS *and* QUAIL *rise, holding each other up.* QUAIL *is limping.*

SASSAFRAS. What's the matter, neighbour Quail?
QUAIL. I've got blisters.
VATZLAV. The rights to property being inviolable and sacred, no one ought to be deprived of it except in cases of evident public necessity, legally ascertained, and on condition of a previous just indemnity.

(SASSAFRAS *and* QUAIL *go out right.* QUAIL *is* *limping. The little curtain disappears into the* *flies.* VATZLAV *goes out following the two* *peasants.*)

SCENE 37

Enter right the GENIUS *and the* GUIDE.

THE GUIDE. This is as far as I can go.

THE GENIUS. Lead me to the other side of the hill. I can find my own way after that.

THE GUIDE. No, I can go no farther.

THE GENIUS. Why not?

THE GUIDE. Because the crest of the hill is the border; on the other side they have orders to castrate all camels.

THE GENIUS. But you're not a camel.

THE GUIDE. It's obvious that you're a stranger to these parts. First they castrate, then they look to see if you're a camel.

THE GENIUS. Why was such an order given?

THE GUIDE. Because it's easier to cut things off than to make them grow.

THE GENIUS. They're right. A camel's possessions are his private property and private property is the curse of society.

THE GUIDE. That's it, sir. And once deprived of his private property the camel is able to hit high notes he would never have attempted before.

THE GENIUS. Then surely he sings hymns to the glory of justice.

> (*A solemn cantata is heard, sung by men with falsetto voices.*)

THE GUIDE. There they come. (*He runs off left.*)
THE GENIUS. I will follow those voices. Guide my steps, sweet music. (*He goes out right.*)

SCENE 38

Enter right MRS BAT *carrying an earthenware pot.*

MRS BAT. I'm in love with the bear. There's no cure for it and I don't want one. If I had a cure, I'd throw it away. I'd burn this whole forest if it contained a balm that could heal my heart. I myself am my sickness, I would die if I were cured. My conscience sermonizes me, but I've left it at home. It's a conscience for home use, and this is the wilderness. What is forbidden in the city is permitted in the forest. The forest is without sin. How can there be sin where there are no men, but only bears?
OEDIPUS (*off*). Wait for me, madam.
MRS BAT. He's found me after all.

SCENE 39

Enter right OEDIPUS.

OEDIPUS. Where are you, madam?

MRS BAT. Here. (*She goes to the other side of the stage.*)

OEDIPUS (*goes to where she was before, looking for her with his cane*). You're not here at all.

MRS BAT. Not there. Here.

(OEDIPUS *goes towards the voice.* MRS BAT *goes back to where she was before.*)

OEDIPUS. She says here when she's there. And when I go there, she's here.

MRS BAT. Not there. (*She takes* OEDIPUS *by the hand and leads him to where she was before.*) Here.

OEDIPUS. Oh, here.

MRS BAT. Here. (*Surprised*) Why, yes, I must have been mistaken.

OEDIPUS (*tapping the pot gently with his cane*). What have you got there, madam?

MRS BAT (*hiding the pot behind her back*). Nothing.

OEDIPUS. In that little pot?

MRS BAT. Nothing.

OEDIPUS. Then what do you need a pot for?

MRS BAT. It's a pot full of nothing.

OEDIPUS. Let me taste it.

MRS BAT. But it's a bitter nothing.

OEDIPUS (*menacingly*). I wish to taste it, madam. (*He*

puts his finger into the pot and licks it.) Mmm ...
it's sweet.

MRS BAT. It's bitter.

OEDIPUS. It's honey, madam.

MRS BAT. Oh. Then it must be sweet.

OEDIPUS. Taking honey to the forest? That's dangerous.

MRS BAT. Who would harm me?

OEDIPUS. The bears.

MRS BAT. Who's that?

OEDIPUS. They love honey.

MRS BAT. Really? I didn't know.

SCENE 40

*Enter BOBBIE from the left in bear mask. He is not seen
by the others.*

OEDIPUS. What is the reason, madam, for this strange
excursion?

MRS BAT. I wish to take the air.

OEDIPUS. All alone?

MRS BAT. Do you know someone who can do my
breathing for me?

OEDIPUS. At this time of day?

MRS BAT. I need air at all hours. It's best at dusk.

OEDIPUS. It will soon be night.

MRS BAT (*retreating slowly to the left on tiptoe*).
Night? What's that to me?

68

OEDIPUS. Don't trifle with the darkness, madam. The forest is always dangerous, but it's most dangerous at night.

MRS BAT. I fear neither the forest nor the darkness. Why should I?

OEDIPUS. Because in the darkness good is indistinguishable from evil.

MRS BAT. That's fine. If I can't see evil, then it won't tempt me.

OEDIPUS. It's not fine at all. In the darkness you can sin without knowing it.

MRS BAT. I don't want to know. (*She goes out left.*)

SCENE 41

OEDIPUS. Oh, madam, madam! I sinned once without knowing it. I was punished with blindness.

BOBBIE. Why were you punished if you didn't know?

OEDIPUS. Because the law is the law. Because I had eyes and I acted like a blind man, I was made blind. Now I'm the guardian of the law.

BOBBIE. What's the good of the law?

OEDIPUS. To safeguard morality.

BOBBIE. What's the good of morality?

OEDIPUS. Our morality is the basis of our civilization.

BOBBIE. But supposing it were the other way around?

Supposing our civilization were the basis of our morality?

OEDIPUS. Our morality would be a necessity, hence all the more justified.

BOBBIE. Then it's moral for my father to drink the blood of the people in broad daylight. If that's morality, the civilization it's based on should rot; no, the morality such a civilization is based on should rot. Or damn it all, let them both rot.

OEDIPUS. What's that you're saying, madam ... Is that your voice?

BOBBIE. No, it's mine.

OEDIPUS. Oh. Then it's a voice that resembles another as a mother's voice resembles her child's.

BOBBIE. Tell me how you sinned.

OEDIPUS. I killed my father and committed incest with my mother.

BOBBIE. Good for you! (*He goes out left.*)

SCENE 42

OEDIPUS. Who said that? (*He gropes around with his cane, and goes out left.*)

Enter from the right SASSAFRAS *and* QUAIL *carrying*
VATZLAV *in a litter consisting of an ornate armchair
slung on two poles.* QUAIL *is limping.*

VATZLAV. These damn woods. They may be all right
for animals but not for honest citizens who've
made a little money by the sweat of their brow.
What do you find in woods like this? Bears and
bandits. The former set a bad example, because
they don't work and own no property, so demon-
strating that it's possible to get by without doing
anything or owning anything. As for the latter, let's
not tempt fate by even mentioning them. There've
been a lot of strangers hanging around here lately,
tramps from God knows where, attracted by the
wealth and freedom of our country. Runaway
slaves. In search of freedom; that's what they say.
But I say: Each man gets only as much freedom
as he deserves. Why were they slaves in their own
country if they deserved any better? (QUAIL
stumbles.) Watch where you step.

QUAIL. I've got a sore foot.

VATZLAV. Who cares?

QUAIL. Don't say that, boss. If all men are equal, my
foot's as good as yours.

SASSAFRAS. You got to be nice to us 'cause we're the
people.

VATZLAV. What makes you so smart all of sudden?

SASSAFRAS. 'Taint me, it was in the paper.

VATZLAV. That's the times for you. Now that they've invented justice, everybody's talking about Quail. Quail is suffering, so you've got to suffer too. You can't even sleep or eat in peace. If you sleep, they tell you, 'Don't sleep, Quail isn't sleeping.' If you eat, 'Don't eat, Quail isn't eating.' The sun sets. 'Don't set, Mr Sun, Quail isn't setting.' A tree blossoms. 'Stop blossoming, Mr Tree, Quail isn't blossoming.' The devil take you and your blossoms.

QUAIL. Don't blaspheme, sir. I don't mind, but if society heard you, they wouldn't like it.

VATZLAV. I'm not afraid of the truth. A fish used to be a fish, a poor man used to be a poor man. When you ate fish, the poor man stood and watched you. Now it's all mixed up. The fish is still a fish, but the poor man is a bone and he sticks in your throat.

SASSAFRAS. That's not the whole of it, boss. They say the fish will eat us all soon, you and us and them.

VATZLAV. The fish? What fish?

SASSAFRAS. The fish Leviathan.

QUAIL. The end of the world.

VATZLAV. When? Now? Just when business was beginning to look up!

(SASSAFRAS *and* QUAIL *go out left carrying* VATZLAV.)

SCENE 44

Enter right MRS BAT *with her pot of honey.*

MRS BAT. My idiotic conscience has warned me of the
night. What difference does it make whether I see
what I'm doing? Besides, I have no intention of
sinning. If I were going to sin, I'd feel ashamed, I'd
hide. If I had evil thoughts, I'd hide my honey. But
I'm not hiding it and that means I'm above sus-
picion. If I had anything to hide, I wouldn't cry
aloud in the forest, I wouldn't tempt the hunger
of the bear. But I do cry out: Honey! Honey!
Come and get it! (*She goes out left.*)

SCENE 45

From the right enter QUAIL *and* SASSAFRAS *carrying*
VATZLAV *in his litter.*

VATZLAV. How can you tell when it's the end of the
world?
SASSAFRAS. First it gets very dark.
VATZLAV. It's getting dark now.
QUAIL. It's not really dark, boss, the moon is rising.
VATZLAV. That's good news.

73

SASSAFRAS. There'll be plenty of light.

VATZLAV. Give me darkness. I wish the moon would go out.

QUAIL. It's not really light, boss. That's not the moon, it's somebody coming with a candle.

SCENE 46

Enter right OEDIPUS *with a lighted candle.*

OEDIPUS. Night has fallen. Anything can happen in the darkness. I've lighted my candle to prevent conscience from falling asleep. Because I know by sad experience how easy it is to sin even with seeing eyes. In the dusk it's still easier, and for sinning the black night is the best time of all.

VATZLAV. A bandit. All shaggy, with evil in his eyes.

(SASSAFRAS *and* QUAIL *drop the litter and fall on their knees before* OEDIPUS.)

SASSAFRAS *and* QUAIL (*in unison*). O saint!

VATZLAV. A saint? Damn near broke my neck with this saintliness. Looks more like a beggar to me. Hey you! No begging around here.

QUAIL. Your blessing.

VATZLAV. Forget it.

OEDIPUS (*goes slowly to the left, tapping his cane on the ground*). I can tell by the voices that here are two pious men and one tightwad. But none of

74

these voices is the voice of that wicked man or that godless woman. I will go my way.

SASSAFRAS (*rising*). He won't give us his blessing.

VATZLAV. He walks like a blind man. But why should a blind man carry a candle? Hey! What are you doing with a candle if you're blind?

OEDIPUS. This candle, sir, protects us all against evil.

VATZLAV. Either he's pretending to be blind, and then he's a crook, or he's really blind, and then he's mad.

OEDIPUS. Woe betide you if it goes out!

VATZLAV. We'll see about that. (*He blows out the candle.*)

OEDIPUS. Shine, candle, shine! (*He goes out left.*)

SCENE 47

VATZLAV. A lunatic. I knew there were bandits and bears in these woods, I'd forgotten about lunatics. What's the matter with you two? You look like door-posts.

SASSAFRAS (*crossing himself*). You blew the saint's candle out.

VATZLAV. So what?

QUAIL (*crossing himself*). Woe betide you!

VATZLAV. Have you both gone crazy? (QUAIL *and* SASSAFRAS *run out to the right.*) Hey, stop ... Wait for me ... Is everybody nuts? (*Hoists the litter on his back and runs after them.*)

SCENE 48

Enter left MR BAT *followed by the* LACKEY.

MR BAT. What seems to be the trouble?
THE LACKEY. In the first place, madame is very much upset.
MR BAT. And in the second place?
THE LACKEY. It seems that the bear is stirring up trouble. He's been speaking with the peasants, inciting them to rebellion.
MR BAT. Tell the foresters to get ready for the hunt. Tell them to round up the hounds and load the guns.

(*The* LACKEY *goes out left.*)

SCENE 49

From the right enter Doggy-woggy.

MR BAT. What do you want, you toady? Can't you keep an eye on your mistress? Do you think I feed you to run loose like a stray? Go find her or I'll make you a watch-dog, and all you'll get to eat is what you can bite out of trespassers. Where's your mistress? You're plotting something, you black bastard. What woods? ... Why in the

woods? ... Sh ... not so loud ... Dog, curly courte-
san, quadruped page, flatterer, tail-wagger, loathsome mutt! If your perfumed snout isn't lying, I'll
reward you with his bones, and a bear has plenty.
You'll be gnawing on them all winter. And his
skin, I'll give you his skin for a bed. But if you've
lied ... (*He picks up Doggy-woggy and shakes him.*)
You'll be sorry, Iago. (*He tosses Doggy-woggy off
stage right. He claps his hands. Enter the* LACKEY.)
Call the hunt!

(MR BAT *and the* LACKEY *go out left.*)

SCENE 50

QUAIL *and* SASSAFRAS *enter from the right. They look
at the sky.*

SASSAFRAS. That's funny. Not a cloud in the sky and
it's dark. It's a long way till night and the stars
are shining. (QUAIL *blows his nose loudly. A flash
of lightning.*) Better cut that out, neighbour.
QUAIL. What did I do?
SASSAFRAS. I dunno. Maybe you're only blowing your
nose, but maybe you're thundering too, and that
makes for lightning.

(QUAIL *blows his nose twice. Two flashes of
lightning.*)

QUAIL. Man!

SASSAFRAS. What did I tell you?

QUAIL. Beats the shit out of me.

SASSAFRAS. Don't worry. There's plenty left.

QUAIL. You know what, neighbour? I'll try it again.

SASSAFRAS. No, don't.

(QUAIL *blows his nose once. They wait. No lightning.*)

QUAIL. Hey. No lightning?

SASSAFRAS. Naw.

QUAIL. But it's getting darker.

(*A violent flash of lightning followed immediately by three claps of thunder resembling three cannon shots.* QUAIL *and* SASSAFRAS *run to the other side of the stage and stop their ears.*)

SASSAFRAS. Quit it, neighbour.

(*A fourth explosion louder than the last.*)

Quit it, I tell you.

QUAIL. 'Taint me. It's him up there.

SASSAFRAS. I don't believe you. I'll never believe you again.

(*They run out left.*)

SCENE 51

The barking of dogs coming closer and closer. VATZLAV *enters running from right, with the litter on his back. His violent movements show that he is being attacked*

78

by the pack. He struggles, kicks, rushes forward, snatches first one leg then the other away from the dogs.

VATZLAV. Get away! Don't touch me. It's all a mistake, Mr Hound. I'm a law-abiding citizen, I pay my taxes. Ouch. Let me go, you cur. That's my leg. Why does the government hire such stupid dogs? Ouch! Ouch! I was joking, Mr Hound. Hunting's all right with me if you hunt the right people. I'm all for it. Get away, you mangy cur! Will you … ? No, he won't. Not my ears! Kindly stick to my legs. Ouch, ouch! Get back, you ugly mutts. No, I didn't mean you, you're the noble descendants of the great whale. I'll put in a complaint. You'll see. I've got witnesses. I've got friends. I've got justice on my side. Ouch! Ouch! I've got children! (*He runs out left. The barking of the pack recedes and dies away.*)

SCENE 52

Enter from the right OEDIPUS and BOBBIE. BOBBIE is wearing the bear mask. OEDIPUS is walking backwards. BOBBIE is holding the point of his sword at OEDIPUS's throat.

BOBBIE. Defend yourself.

OEDIPUS. If you have a conscience …

BOBBIE. Defend yourself.

OEDIPUS. I will not defend myself, I will defend the law …

BOBBIE. Defend yourself.

> (*They take the attitudes of fencers. Awkwardly* OEDIPUS *crosses his white cane with* BOBBIE'S *sword.* BOBBIE *could easily strike the cane from the blind man's hand, but he seems to derive pleasure from his superiority. He repeatedly allows* OEDIPUS *to recover his guard, then attacks again and knocks the cane aside, laughing. Still fencing, they both go out right.*)

SCENE 53

The barking of dogs. VATZLAV *enters running from the right, with his litter on his back. He is out of breath. He puts the litter on the ground and sits down on it to get his breath.*

VATZLAV. Come to think of it, they're right. Animals are smart. They smelled a foreigner. Who should they bite? Not one of their own people. If I were in their place, I'd start with myself too, and leave the natives for later. But that's no help, because I'm not in their place.

(*The pack approaches.*)
Christ, here they come again. (*He puts the litter
on his back and runs off left.*)

SCENE 54

Enter from the right BOBBIE *in bear mask and* MR BAT;
they fight violently with swords. MR BAT *is obviously
the stronger and* BOBBIE *retreats. They go out left.*

SCENE 55

Enter right the LACKEY, *running.*

THE LACKEY. Master! Master! (*He runs out left.*)

SCENE 56

Enter from the right MRS BAT *dressed like a comic-
opera gypsy. She is holding a tambourine with which
she accompanies her speech.*

MRS BAT. I'll teach my bear to dance and we'll go everywhere together. We'll go from city to city, the good folk won't refuse us their charity. We will go to baptisms and weddings, dances and fairs, but we'll keep away from funerals, fires and public executions. We shall also give churches, cathedrals and convents a wide berth because the Church doesn't approve of us. We shall avoid legislatures, judges, courthouses and district attorneys, in short, all persons and institutions engaged in making laws or enforcing them. We shall have to beware of devoted mothers, stern fathers and obedient children, because, out of their hatred for their own devotion, sternness and obedience, they would be only too eager to turn us over to the above-mentioned institutions. We shall have to distrust those doctors who busy themselves with mental health; they would try to persuade us that we're sick. And poets : they would want to make us believe in tragedy. Yes, we shall have to distrust poets, priests and doctors, because if we reject sickness, tragedy and sin they will call the police. To recapitulate : if we steer clear of doctors, poets, judges, legislators, ecclesiastics, mothers, fathers and children, not to mention divine, human and natural morality, nothing can happen to us. We shall be happy. (*She goes out left.*)

SCENE 57

VATZLAV *enters right with his litter. He looks round,*
listens in all four directions. He puts the litter down,
climbs up on it, looks round and listens.

VATZLAV. I don't hear them any more. Where are
they? I don't get it. What's going to happen now?
Yes, they took a few chunks out of me, but at
least they protected me against the thieves, ped-
dlers and agitators who are always trying to make
off with what you've earned by your honest toil.
I'd rather be bitten now and then than go without
their protection. Yes, little dogs, where are you?
If it weren't for you, wild boars, badgers and all
sorts of forest riffraff would multiply like rabbits.
Maybe they won't be gone for long. Let's not give
up hope, but in the meantime let's try to find a
safe place for our property. (*He loads the litter on
his back and goes off left.*)

SCENE 58

Enter from the right BOBBIE *and* MR BAT. *They are*
still fighting, but now MR BAT *is retreating. They go*
out left.

SCENE 59

The LACKEY *enters from the right, running with a limp. His face is blackened, his clothes torn.*

THE LACKEY. Master, oh, master ... (*He goes out left.*)

SCENE 60

Enter from the right QUAIL *and* SASSAFRAS. *They are carrying bundles containing all their worldly goods.*

SASSAFRAS. All this on account of your cold.

QUAIL. I'm better now.

SASSAFRAS. Sure, now that my house has burned down.

QUAIL. Mine's burned down too. Fire's bad.

SASSAFRAS. Yeah, fire's bad. But it doesn't come up to a good flood.

QUAIL. Or hail.

SASSAFRAS. What do you think of the plague?

QUAIL. You're so picky and choosy. I take what I get.

SASSAFRAS. 'Cause you're ignorant.

(*They go out left.*)

SCENE 61

Enter right MR BAT *and* BOBBIE, *fighting fiercely.*
BOBBIE *retreats. They go out left, fighting.*

SCENE 62

The LACKEY *enters right, staggering. He crosses the*
stage slowly, falls, crawls a few feet, then stops still
and dies. From the right enter two SOLDIERS *and the*
OFFICER. *They have on helmets with wide rims, coats*
of mail, tight-fitting breeches. The SOLDIERS *carry*
lances, the OFFICER *a sword.*

THE OFFICER. Remove this body.
> (*The* SOLDIERS *carry the* LACKEY *out left, fol-*
> *lowed by the* OFFICER.)

SCENE 63

VATZLAV (*off*). Fire! Fire! Help! Help! (VATZLAV
enters right, dragging his litter.) Oh, my years of

bitter toil, oh, my property! (*He takes off his hat and beats the chair with it as though to put out the fire.*)

SCENE 64

Enter from the right GENERAL BARBARO. *Helmet and golden coat of mail, sword. Behind him a* SOLDIER *carrying at the end of a pole the mummified* GENIUS. *With one finger of his upraised hand the* GENIUS *is pointing the way. His face is waxen white, on his cheeks two red circles. Lips heavily rouged. Round his neck a wreath of paper roses. Over his head a golden halo. Behind him* DRUMMERS *and* LANCERS. *The detachment stops.* VATZLAV *puts on his hat and hides under his chair.*

BARBARO. That does it, men. The war's over. I always said these degenerates would be a pushover.

SCENE 65

Enter QUAIL *and* SASSAFRAS *from the left escorted by* SOLDIERS *who prod them in the back with their lances.*

SASSAFRAS. How's it going, neighbour Quail?

QUAIL. I've got shooting pains in the back.

SASSAFRAS. I've been having little twinges myself.

QUAIL. We must have caught cold.

BARBARO. Who are you?

QUAIL. I'm Quail. This is Sassafras.

BARBARO. I didn't ask for your names. Are you rich or poor?

QUAIL. We're poor, boss.

BARBARO. Lucky for you. We have come to liberate you. Help the poor, destroy the rich, as our Beloved Leader has taught us. (*He bows low to the mummy.*) May he live for ever! (*He raises his hand as though to strike the* SOLDIER *who is hold-*
- *ing the mummy.*) Is that the way to hold him?

(*Frightened, the* SOLDIER *raises the pole higher.*)
That's it. Well, what do you think of him?

QUAIL. Pretty.

SASSAFRAS. But kind of stiff.

BARBARO. I beg your pardon?

SASSAFRAS. Kind of lifeless.

BARBARO (*putting his sword to* SASSAFRAS'*s throat*). I didn't quite get that.

SASSAFRAS. Lively, that's the word. Bless my soul. I never saw anybody looking so lively.

QUAIL. In the pink.

BARBARO (*lowering his sword*). That's better. (*He picks his ear with his finger.*) Sometimes I'm deaf in my left ear. He's lively all right and what's more he's alive. We've just embalmed him a little to keep

87

him from spoiling. The surface may be a bit shiny but it keeps out the rain. In all other respects, he's in good health, better than you ... And smart! He knows everything. (*To the* SOLDIER.) Higher, you jackass!

SCENE 66

MR BAT, *unarmed, is led in from the left by a* SOLDIER.

BARBARO. Who's this?

THE SOLDIER. Mr Bat, the capitalist. He sucked the blood of the people.

BARBARO (*to* QUAIL *and* SASSAFRAS). Is that true?

QUAIL. Yessir, he sure did.

SASSAFRAS. An all-day sucker, that's what he was.

BARBARO. Hang him.

SASSAFRAS. Long live!

BARBARO. The capitalist?

QUAIL. Of course not, boss. He meant the hangman.

BARBARO. Oh, that's different.

QUAIL. He knows the score. Don't you, Sassafras?

SASSAFRAS. Sure thing. No use long-living a man with a rope around his neck.

BARBARO. Hm, you seem to have a head on your shoulders.

SASSAFRAS. That's right, boss. We're the people. That's the wisdom of the people.

QUAIL. Comes with our mother's milk, boss.

BARBARO. Go in peace. And never forget: you've been liberated by the liberators.

QUAIL (*bowing*). Thanks, boss.

SASSAFRAS (*bowing*). Thank you kindly, boss.

BARBARO. Take this man to the gallows.

(*The* SOLDIER *goes out left with* MR BAT.)

QUAIL. Let's get out of here, Sassafras. From now on we'll just have to suck our own blood.

SASSAFRAS. Got to keep up with the times.

(*They go out left.*)

SCENE 67

BARBARO (*to the* SOLDIERS *who had brought in* QUAIL *and* SASSAFRAS). Hang those fellows too. (*The* SOLDIERS *start left.*) ... But cut the rope, that'll teach them gratitude. First you hang them, then you cut the rope. They're too smart. That'll take them down a peg.

(*The* SOLDIERS *go out left.*)

SCENE 68

From the left the two SOLDIERS *bring in* BOBBIE *who is wearing the bear mask but is no longer armed.*

BARBARO. Who are you?

BOBBIE. The bear.

BARBARO. I say you're a camel.

BOBBIE. Have I got a hump?

BARBARO. How do I know? Maybe you haven't. And maybe you have. If you have, you must be hiding it, because I don't see it. In that case you're circumventing the authorities. And if you haven't got a hump ... how do I know you wouldn't have hidden it if you had one? In either case you're guilty because in the present period everybody's circumventing the authorities or trying to. So to be on the safe side, we'll put you down as a camel.

BOBBIE. I am a wild, free and independent bear, and I recognize no authority.

BARBARO. That proves he's a camel.

BOBBIE. I serve no man.

BARBARO. A camel if ever there was one.

BOBBIE. Down with authority.

BARBARO. Definitely a camel. (*To the* SOLDIERS) Cut off his camelhood. This camel's voice is too deep.

　　　(*Two* SOLDIERS *lead* BOBBIE *out left.*)

SCENE 69

Two SOLDIERS *enter from the left leading* OEDIPUS.

OEDIPUS. I wish to make a complaint.

BARBARO. Go right ahead, old man. I like denunciations.

OEDIPUS. A young man wants to kill his father and violate his mother.

BARBARO. Must be full of beans.

OEDIPUS. Which is contrary to divine, human and natural law.

BARBARO. Wait a minute. Who are you?

OEDIPUS. I am the exemplar of divine, human and natural law.

BARBARO. That's quite a mouthful ... (*He makes himself comfortable in the chair under which* VATZLAV *is hiding.*) Hm. You must be a V.I.P.

OEDIPUS. Yes, indeed. An indispensable model to all mankind.

BARBARO. An official personage, so to speak.

OEDIPUS. Upon my shoulders rests the order of the world.

BARBARO. Are you as important as a king?

OEDIPUS. I was a king but I renounced my kingdom to become guardian of the law. It follows that my office is the highest of all human dignities.

BARBARO (*leaning back in his chair*). You mean you're

more important than me? Holier than our Beloved Leader?

OEDIPUS. No one is holier than I.

BARBARO (*to the* SOLDIERS). Boys, take care of the senior citizen. Teach him the realities of life. Let's go, boys. I want to see teamwork.

OEDIPUS. What does this mean?

BARBARO. It means they're going to bugger you.

OEDIPUS. I am Oedipus Rex.

BARBARO. We don't care if you're Santa Claus. With God's help we've fucked better people than you. Haven't we, boys?

THE SOLDIERS. Hoorah!

BARBARO. See? Don't worry. They'll fix you up.

OEDIPUS. Violate me? Me, an old man?

BARBARO. That's the way it is.

OEDIPUS. Will the heavens not take pity? Will the sun not go out and darkness fall upon the earth? … Between you and me, what pleasure … ?

BARBARO. Who said anything about pleasure? Take a look at yourself. We're doing it for the glory of the flag and to demonstrate our virility which shrinks from nothing, not even from you. We fear no sacrifice. We'll bugger you with tears in our eyes, but we'll bugger you. Right boys?

THE SOLDIERS. Hoorah!

OEDIPUS. Why this sacrifice?

BARBARO. To humble your pride. (*He stands up.*) So you were a king? An examplar? A V.I.P.? Splendid. I'm glad you're not some poor bastard. A venerable

patriarch? That's perfect. Today my soldiers are
going to bugger you. A hero of art and sculpture?
They'll bugger the sculpture out of you. A guardian
of the law? The conscience of mankind? A good
stiff cock up your ass will knock that out of you.
Show you who's running things around here. (*He
sits down.*) Let's go, boys. Take him away.

OEDIPUS. Woe is me!

> (*Drums. Two* SOLDIERS *seize the old man under
> the arms and drag him out left. The whole de-
> tachment goes out after him as the drums roll.
> The bearer of the mummy closes the procession.*
> BARBARO *stretches, yawns and falls asleep in his
> chair, without dropping his sword.*)

SCENE 70

VATZLAV *issues cautiously from his hiding place. He
looks around him on all sides. He stops in front of the
sleeping* BARBARO.

VATZLAV. He's asleep. Made himself comfortable ...
In my place. I bet he feels pretty good. I wonder
what he's dreaming about. Before he took my
place, he could dream about taking it. What can
he dream about now? About losing it. Conclusion :
he had pleasanter dreams before. I could feel sorry

for him, except that he's having his bad dreams sitting down, while I'm making a good speech standing up.

(BARBARO *moves restlessly in his sleep and sighs.*) All right, sigh. Your conscience must be tormenting you for taking my chair. A nightmare. It must be killing you. I'd give it a hand, except you might wake up, the nightmare would vanish and I'd be left holding the bag. But the more I look at your thieving mug, the more I want to fix it for you. I'd better look at something else. Another minute and I won't be able to resist. (*He turns his head, then looks back at* BARBARO, *then looks away again.*) No, a little patience. (*He looks.*) I can feel myself slipping. (*He turns his head.*) Don't look. Don't look ... (*He looks.*) Or I'll bash his head in ... (*He turns away and puts his hands over his eyes.*) Don't look, don't look ... (*He looks and raises his hand to strike.*)

(BARBARO *shifts his position. Frightened,* VATZLAV *jumps back.* BARBARO *goes on sleeping.*)

Whew! Narrow escape you had there. Oh well, maybe it's good he's asleep. He's not nice when he's awake. I'll let him sleep, just take back my property. But how? First I'll disarm him. Then we'll see. (*He touches* BARBARO's *hand, tries to take the sword.* BARBARO *grunts in his sleep. Frightened,* VATZLAV *jumps back.*) All right, all right. I'm not interested in your property. Just return mine and we'll call it square. Nothing to get sore about.

Come on. Hell, he won't listen to reason. (*He takes* BARBARO *by one leg and tries to pull him off the chair. Every time* BARBARO *moves or grunts,* VATZLAV *stops, puts a finger on his lips and tries to soothe* BARBARO *as if he were a child having bad dreams. Finally, half off the chair,* BARBARO *moves so violently that* VATZLAV *gives up.*) Is he stubborn! Oh no, my fine-feathered friend, don't think you can disinherit me so easily. Hanging people, cutting things off of people, okay, that's your business. But my property is my property. Give it back. (*He approaches the chair from behind, seizes the end of the poles, raises the litter with* BARBARO *in it and drags it to the right like a wheelbarrow.* BARBARO *slips to the ground. Suddenly he jumps up with his feet together and immediately assumes a fencer's position. But he doesn't know where his adversary is and does not see* VATZLAV.*)

BARBARO. Ho, guards!

(*Three* SOLDIERS *run in, two from the left, one from the right, with lances lowered. They surround* VATZLAV, *touching him symmetrically with their lances.* VATZLAV *raises his hands.* BARBARO *approaches him and examines him attentively.*)

Are you one of us?

(VATZLAV *shakes his head.*)

Where do you belong?

VATZLAV. I'm a foreigner.

BARBARO. He's too thin to be from here, but too fat to be one of us. With the new regime, of course, the natives will get thin and we'll get fat, but then he'll be too fat for a native and too thin to be one of us. I'd better hold him until tomorrow. If by then he hasn't definitely gained or lost weight, we'll hand him over to the executioner. Because a man has got to belong somewhere.

(*He sits down in the litter. Two* SOLDIERS *pick it up – to avoid being encumbered by their lances they pass them along the poles of the litter or sling them on their backs. They go out left, carrying* BARBARO. VATZLAV *follows them, escorted by a third* SOLDIER.

SCENE 71

Enter from the right QUAIL *and* SASSAFRAS, *each with a rope around his neck. The ropes are of equal length and trail on the ground.*

SASSAFRAS. All this talk about equality. And now your rope is longer than mine.
QUAIL. That's impossible.
SASSAFRAS. Why is it impossible?
QUAIL. Because yours is longer.
SASSAFRAS. I'd give you the shirt off my back, but

if they hang us equal they should cut us down
equal. It ain't right your having more rope.

QUAIL. I don't know about that. What bugs me is
having less.

SASSAFRAS. Give back the difference.

QUAIL. You give back the difference.

SASSAFRAS. If that's the way it is, if you won't do
what's right, I'm going to complain to our liber-
ator. Good man! He strung us up in equality.

QUAIL. Good idea. He'll cut your rope down to size.

SASSAFRAS. He won't let me get the short end.

QUAIL and SASSAFRAS (in unison). He will do justice!
(They go out left.)

SCENE 72

VATZLAV *enters right. He is dressed as at the beginning
of the play in a shirt and tattered pants. He has neither
his blazer nor bowler nor watch nor ring, but he still
has his shoes. He is followed by the* EXECUTIONER *in
red tights, his face covered by a red hood. He is carrying a large double-edged sword pointed upward.*

VATZLAV. Somebody hasn't kept his word in this deal.
It could be Providence or it could be me. No, come
to think of it, that's not it. We made a pact. We
both did what we were supposed to, and nothing

came of it. I wanted to be free, rich and happy, and I haven't really succeeded, though no one would deny that I've had my freedom, that I've had money off and on and been happy from time to time. So I can't find fault with Providence, but I've nothing much to thank it for either. I've been free as often as not free, glutted as often as hungry, happy as often as sad; for a time I was young and now I'm old. I've gone in and out of the house an equal number of times, I've been awake and I've slept, done a certain amount of loving and a certain amount of hating. All in all, it's time to break up my partnership with Providence, because it hasn't done either of us any good, and retire from business, because the debt cancels out the credit. Altogether, living is an ungrateful profession. And now they want me to be a professional corpse. But taken as a profession, death is just as stupid as life. What I'd like is amateur status : I wouldn't mind dying now and then, any more than I'd mind living, what I object to is sinking my whole capital into either one of them. These new bosses seem to attach a great deal of importance to my execution, they're determined to have me for a partner. But dying to order doesn't appeal to me; it would tie me up for all eternity. So I'll turn down their offer and clear out of this shop where I don't want to buy anything and have nothing to sell.

(*He takes out a cardboard jumping-jack, pulls*

*the string and the jumping-jack moves. He shows
it to the* EXECUTIONER, *who looks at the toy with
interest and laughs good-naturedly. He holds out
his hand,* VATZLAV *gives him the jumping-jack.
The* EXECUTIONER *holds it by the top string but
the sword in his other hand prevents him from
pulling the bottom string. Eager to oblige,* VATZ-
LAV *pulls the string, the jumping-jack moves,
the* EXECUTIONER *laughs. He gives* VATZLAV *his
sword to hold. Now, with both hands free, he
works the jumping-jack by himself and laughs
aloud.* VATZLAV *tiptoes backward to the right,
turns and runs out. The* EXECUTIONER *plays for
another few minutes, then suddenly notices that
his victim has disappeared and stops laughing.
With an inarticulate cry of rage, he dashes off
in pursuit of* VATZLAV. *He runs out roaring.)*

SCENE 73

Enter from the right MRS BAT *in deep mourning. She
is leading* BOBBIE-BEAR *by the hand. Little red bows
and silver bells are attached to his hands and feet.*
MRS BAT *has a tambourine with which she beats time.*
BOBBIE *does an awkward bear dance. From the left
enters* VATZLAV *running, the* EXECUTIONER'S *sword
over his shoulder.*

MRS BAT (*holding out the tambourine to* VATZLAV. *In a plaintive voice*). Alms for the poor bear and his keeper!

(VATZLAV *stops, looks in his pockets, finds a coin, tosses it into the tambourine, and runs out right.* MRS BAT *moves left, shaking the tambourine,* BOBBIE-BEAR *dancing beside her. Enter from the left the* EXECUTIONER *holding a rope ending in a noose.*)

MRS BAT (*to the* EXECUTIONER). Alms for the poor bear. (*Paying no attention, the* EXECUTIONER *runs out right.* MRS BAT *and* BOBBIE-BEAR *go out left.*)

SCENE 74

Enter from the right SASSAFRAS *and* QUAIL *with their ropes around their necks.* VATZLAV *runs in from the left with the sword over his shoulder.*

QUAIL. Hey, boss.

SASSAFRAS. Wait, boss.

(VATZLAV *waits.*)

QUAIL. Settle our argument.

SASSAFRAS. Who's got the longer rope?

QUAIL. Him!

SASSAFRAS. Him!

VATZLAV. Since you both think the other's rope is

longer, swap ropes and don't bother me. I'm in a
hurry. If I waste time on your ropes, I'll get one all
to myself and I won't even have time to see if it's
longer than yours.

SASSAFRAS. What's that? Longer?

QUAIL. Longer than ours?

SASSAFRAS. Oh no, you don't.

QUAIL. Get him, neighbour.

> (*They jump on* VATZLAV, *throw his sword on
> the ground and beat him. Enter the* EXECUTIONER
> *from the left with his rope.* VATZLAV *tears him-
> self free and runs out right, with the* EXECU-
> TIONER *behind him.* QUAIL *and* SASSAFRAS *go out
> left, shaking their fists at* VATZLAV.)

SCENE 75

Enter VATZLAV *from the left, breathing heavily, with
his hand on his heart.*

VATZLAV. Whew ... I've shaken him off. That's not
surprising, I've had more training in running away
than he has in running after. High time. I can't go
any farther. When I think of all the running away
I've done in my life! But this time my training
won't help me, because here I am back on the
beach. The waves dash against the shore, the gulls

cry, not a ship in sight. But what good is all this empty space if I can't go on? (*He sits down facing the sea upstage. He puts his hand over his eyes and views the horizon.*)

SCENE 76

To the left a woman is heard moaning and weeping. Enter JUSTINE. *She no longer has her wreath, her hair is in disarray, her dress dirty and torn. In her arms she is carrying a baby. She moves right.*

VATZLAV. Hey!
>(JUSTINE *stops, turns towards* VATZLAV *and stops crying.*)
>Say, I know you. Aren't you the daughter of that old codger who invented Justice?

JUSTINE. No.

VATZLAV. What do you mean, no? He gave you the name of Justice and made you exhibit yourself to the common herd. I made a pile of money on it.

JUSTINE. It wasn't me.

VATZLAV. Maybe not. You didn't have a baby then. (*He gets up, approaches* JUSTINE, *bends over the baby.* JUSTINE *looks away.*) Let's see. Don't be ashamed. Hm ... he reminds me of somebody too. Who's the happy father?

JUSTINE. The father is happy, the mother is unhappy.

VATZLAV. Really? Why?

JUSTINE. I didn't want to be a mother.

VATZLAV. Then how come ...

JUSTINE. I didn't know where babies came from.

VATZLAV. Where did you think they came from?

JUSTINE. The head.

VATZLAV. The head?

JUSTINE. By the workings of reason.

VATZLAV. The poor thing is off her rocker.

JUSTINE. Daddy told me to watch the birds and the flowers ... It's the same with them ... Nature is reasonable ... I begot you with my head and bore you with my head ... I was going to be a queen ... (*She weeps.*)

VATZLAV. Come on, take it easy ... (*Aside*) That's it, she's wacky.

JUSTINE (weeping). The world is reasonable ...

VATZLAV. Reasonable? The world?

JUSTINE. That's what I thought ... (*She weeps.*)

VATZLAV. Poor thing. Where are you going now with the fruit of your father's wisdom?

JUSTINE. To see the little fishes.

VATZLAV. You're going to drown it?

JUSTINE. The little fishes are reasonable too. They won't do her any harm.

VATZLAV. Give the bastard to me! (*He snatches the baby away from her.*) Hey! Where are you going?

JUSTINE. I'm going to tell the little birds my troubles. (*She runs out left.*)

SCENE 77

VATZLAV. Birds and fishes! What am I going to do with this kid? I've got nothing for her to eat. And besides, I hate babies. (*A police whistle is heard on the left.*) Maybe I could tell them I'm a nursing mother? The benefits of progress, I'll tell them. See, I've had a baby. Why wouldn't they believe me since they believe in progress, reason and justice? Except that they'll kill me, kid and all. (*He goes upstage, stops, faces the sea and addresses the baby.*) See the other shore? Neither do I. But if we could get there, you might grow up to be somebody. Not here. (*A second blast from the police whistle.*) I've heard that a whole people passed through the sea dryshod and reached the other shore. (*A third blast of the whistle. Holding the baby in one arm, VATZLAV takes off his shoes and rolls up his trousers. Then holding his shoes in one hand and the baby in the other, he descends from the far end of the platform with the movements of a man going into the water.*) Brrr ... It's cold. (*He stops. Visible from the waist up, he turns towards the audience.*) You wait here. If I don't come back, you'll know I've made it. Then you can follow. (*Slowly he disappears behind the platform.*)

BIBLIOGRAPHY

The principal works of Slawomir Mrozek, with the dates of their first appearance

Novels
Maleńkie lato (A TINY SUMMER) (Wydawnictwo Literackie, Cracow, 1956)
Ucieczka na poludnie (THE FLIGHT TO THE SOUTH) (Iskry, Warsaw, 1961)

Short Stories
Słoń (THE ELEPHANT) (W.L., Cracow, 1957); translated as 'The Elephant' by Konrad Syrop (London, Macdonald, 1962)
Wesele w Atomicach (THE WEDDING AT ATOMVILLE) (W.L., Cracow, 1959)
Deszcz (RAIN) (W.L., Cracow, 1962)

Cartoons, Satire
Polska w obrazach (POLAND IN PICTURES) (WAG, Cracow, 1957)
Postępowiec (THE PROGRESSIVE) (Iskry, Warsaw, 1960)

Plays
All Mr Mrozek's plays have appeared in the Polish magazine *Dialog*, beginning with *Policja* (THE POLICE) in no. 6, 1958.
Ten plays: *Policja* (THE POLICE); *Męczeństwo Piotra*

Ohey'a (THE MARTYRDOM OF PETER OHEY); *Indyk* (THE TURKEY); *Na pelnym morzu* (OUT AT SEA); *Karol* (CHARLIE); *Strip-tease* (STRIP-TEASE); *Zabawa* (THE PARTY); *Kynolog w rozterce* (THE DOG-BREEDER'S DILEMMA); *Czarowna noc* (ENCHANTED NIGHT) and *Śmierć porucznika* (DEATH OF THE LIEUTENANT) were published in: *Utwory sceniczne* (W.L., Cracow, 1963). Six of these were translated by Nicholas Bethell in *Six Plays* (Cape, 1967).

Tango (TANGO) (*Dialog*, no. 11, 1964)

Poczwórka (QUARTET) (*Dialog*, no. 1, 1967)

Dom na granicy (A HOUSE AT THE FRONTIER) (*Dialog*, no. 5, 1967)

Woda (WATER) (*Dialog*, no. 6, 1967)

Testarium (*Dialog*, no. 11, 1967)

THE AUTHOR

Slawomir Mrozek was born in Bozerzin, near Cracow, on June 26th, 1930. His father was a Post Office official. He studied architecture, painting and Orientalism for a few terms. His first job was on a Cracow newspaper as a writer and cartoonist. While still a journalist, he began to write satirical short stories and it was with a first collection of these, *The Elephant*, that he achieved an early success. These stories were followed by others, by a book of cartoons – *Poland in Pictures* – and by a work which combined his literary and graphic talents: a lampoon on journalism entitled *The Progressive*.

He abandoned journalism in the late 'fifties and his first play, called *The Police*, was first performed in 1958. Eight more short plays followed before he wrote *Tango*, his first full-length play, first performed in 1964. This has been staged in Poland, Germany, Great Britain, France, Italy and Yugoslavia and a number of other countries.

Most of Mrozek's plays have been performed on the B.B.C. Third Programme, on television and in Edinburgh and many other provincial cities. *Tango* was produced by the Royal Shakespeare Company at the Aldwych, London, in 1966. The Polish Contemporary Theatre brought two plays of his in Polish to the Aldwych in the 1964 World Theatre season.

CAPE EDITIONS